JESUS IS LORD

Paul's Life in Christ

JESUS IS LORD

Paul's Life in Christ

by

Joseph Blenkinsopp

PAULIST PRESS DEUS BOOKS

NEW YORK   GLEN ROCK   WESTMINSTER
TORONTO   AMSTERDAM

A Deus Books Edition of the Paulist Press, 1967, by special arrangement with Darton, Longman & Todd, Ltd., London.

NIHIL OBSTAT:
Ricardus J. Foster, S.T.L., L.S.S.
Censor Deputatus

IMPRIMATUR:
✠ Franciscus Grimshaw
Archiepiscopus Birminghamiensis

December 11, 1964

The *Nihil Obstat* and *Imprimatur* are official declarations that a book or pamphlet is free of doctrinal or moral errors. No implication is contained therein that those who have granted the *Nihil Obstat* and *Imprimatur* agree with the contents, opinions or statements expressed.

Published by Paulist Press:
Editorial Office: 304 W. 58th St., N. Y., N. Y. 10019
Business Office: Glen Rock, New Jersey 07452

Manufactured in the United States of America
by Our Sunday Visitor Press

Contents

The Author

Joseph Blenkinsopp was born in 1927. After studies in modern literature at London University, he completed his theological studies in Turin and frequented the Biblical Institute in Rome. He was professor of sacred scripture at the Salesian International Theological College at Melchet Court, England until 1962, and later taught scripture at the Catholic University of Guatemala. He has participated in archaeological work in Palestine, is the noted author of *The Corinthian Mirror* and *The Promise to David,* and contributes to the *Journal of Biblical Literature, Biblica, Catholic Biblical Quarterly* and various other journals.

Acknowledgments

Grateful acknowledgment is made to Rev. Hubert Richards and Joseph Rhymer for valuable comment on the manuscript.

Preface

WE hardly do justice to our faith by studying it as if it were a static system, either in the line of liturgy or theology, much less by thinking of it just as a moral code. Going into the life of Paul is a good way of uncovering the dynamics of the Christian life, the faith in action. This has as its starting point not some theoretical idea or other but *an experience, the experience of the Lord crucified but now risen, alive, present to us in community*. Hence the importance of Paul's conversion, the basic experience of his life (Part I).

This explains how the earliest Christian message centers round the death and resurrection of the Lord, and Paul and his fellow-missionaries inherited that message, though it came to him independently also. In the light of what God had done in the Christ-event, the scriptures (the Old Testament) which Paul had read and grappled with for years suddenly appeared as a drama leading up to this, the last act, with God himself the protagonist. Man's part was to accept this through faith and realize in his own life the mystery of death and resurrection (Part II).

Paul might not have had a very comfortable life but he could hardly have complained that it was unexciting. His hardships were, however, no more than incidental to his missionary work, the result of an invincible, expansive force. Reliving the mission of the Antioch Church and the expeditions which followed takes us to the heart of what being a Christian means better than a library of theology books (Part III); it shows us, moreover, that the end of all this activity was to set up communities of dedicated men and women committed to Christ, living the new life, the first of a new humanity. In a fragmentary and unsystematic way, the extant letters of Paul tell us about that life, what living it implied and where it was all leading (Part IV). They can communicate to us the spirit behind that life and help us to sort out what is essential from what is marginal and secondary (Part V). Little is known of the last years of the life of this extraordinary man (Part VI).

Part I
Paul the Man

THE subject of our study is an Asian Jew who was executed outside the walls of Rome almost exactly nineteen hundred years ago. The number of commemorations held in recent years, the massive sales of new translations of his letters, even his reaching the front page of *Time* (April 18, 1960) go to show his abiding interest and significance even after nineteen hundred years have passed. Even admitting this, though, we might wonder how many people are very familiar with him as a real person or have made a serious effort to read his letters—apart from the odd passages which are used in the Epistle at Mass. There might be more than one reason for this. One modern scholar points out: "Paul is regarded today by many as gloomy as well as great,"[1] and he demands serious attention and thought, since he wrote for people willing to grapple with the deep problems of life. The difficulties are real enough— St. Peter's remark about the letters: "There are some things in them hard to understand" (II Peter 3:16) might be taken as the understatement of the (first) century—but what must strike us, if we make the attempt

[1] Adolph Deissmann in *Paul: A Study in Social and Religious History,* Harper Torchbook, ed. 1957, p. 4. He goes on: "But the darkness is largely due to the bad lamps in our studies, and the modern condemnations of the Apostle as an obscurantist who corrupted the simple gospel of the Nazarene with harsh and difficult dogmas, are the dregs of doctrinaire study of Paul, mostly in the tired brains of gifted amateurs."

with some courage and sympathy, is how approachable, how real and even, to put it tritely, how modern Paul seems.

He first appears on the scene on the occasion of a judicial murder to which he himself was a party. The victim was Stephen, leader of the Hellenist or Greek section of the early Christian community. We are not given an exact date but it was not long after the crucifixion; it may have been made possible or at least easy by the temporary gap in political power occasioned by the recall of Pilate in A.D. 36, though some would prefer an earlier date. At any rate, Paul had probably been among those who had disputed with Stephen in the synagogue of the Cilicians at Jerusalem but "could not withstand the wisdom and the Spirit with which he spoke." We do not know what effect Stephen's magnificent and panoramic reinterpretation of Judaism, his ensuing death and his noble forgiving of his enemies— including Paul—had upon this "young man" who stood by missing nothing. We shall have to come back to this at a later stage.

All that we know about Paul comes from the "Acts" written by Luke who knew him well, being his traveling companion, fellow-missionary and perhaps personal physician, helped out by one or two autobiographical passages in his extant correspondence. Later writings such as *The Acts of Paul* with their fanciful stories about Thecla of Konya (Iconium) really belong to the class of fiction, though they may have preserved an historical tradition here and there.[2] He was born, not

---

[2] The physical description of Paul we find in this work is not particularly flattering: "A man rather small in size, with meeting eyebrows, a rather large nose, baldheaded, bow-legged. Strongly built, he was full of grace for at times he looked like

like Jesus and the apostles in a village or country town, but in a city and remained a city man all his life. He was evidently no recluse but fully familiar with the world of his contemporaries at all levels. Not only could he move in the highest ranks of Roman officialdom; he must have been a familiar figure in the back streets of more than one great city of the Empire and was in and out of jail with some regularity for one long period of his life. He resists all efforts to put him into a fixed category, either psychological, social or religious—but perhaps we could sum up the externals of his life by considering him as Roman, Greek and Jew. Let us examine these three aspects for a moment.

Paul the Roman

In the first place, *he started off in life with the great social and political advantage of Roman citizenship, the* status symbol of that time. He was not just Saul the Jew brought up in the Tarsus ghetto, he was Paulus the *civis Romanus*. Whether or not it was his father who obtained this privilege—either by buying it or in exchange for services rendered—we do not know; but he must have been a person of some social standing. Roman citizenship conferred three rights: *ius suffragii, ius honorum, ius provocandi*. We know nothing of whether or how Paul exercised his right to vote, but the second included immunity from degrading punishments and we see him in Philippi enforcing an apology from the magistrates for having him beaten without a trial, and later on in Jerusalem he narrowly escaped a flogging by insisting on this right. It was during his pre-

a man, at times like an angel." There is some confirmation for one or two aspects of this description in the frescos of the Roman catacombs, beginning in the fourth century.

liminary hearing before Festus the new governor which took place in Caesarea on the coast, Roman headquarters in Palestine, that Paul, as a last resort and practically in despair, made use of the third privilege and demanded to be tried in Nero's supreme court of appeal at Rome (Acts 25:11), and he is still in Rome waiting for his trial when the story breaks off.[3] It is possible that this appeal was a tactical error on Paul's part for, as King Agrippa pointed out after the hearing: "This man could have been set free if he had not appealed to Caesar" (Acts 26:32); but Paul knew his fellow-Jews better than the Romans or Agrippa did and it is equally possible that his refusal to do so might have brought Luke's story to an even more abrupt termination.

Rome, the imperial city and capital of the civilized world, seems to have played a decisive role in Paul's missionary program right from the start, since his deliberate and audacious progress from East to West looks suspiciously like a preconceived plan of conquest for Christ. It is significant here that he makes his most complete statement on the Christian life to the Roman community, one which he had not founded (this was entirely exceptional for him) and tells them how he had wanted right from the beginning to visit them (Romans 1:13–15). Luke begins his story of the early Church in Jerusalem and ends it in Rome because it was there that his future lay, the future into which God was already guiding the Christian commonwealth born on the first Pente-

[3] It has been suggested, not unreasonably, that Acts was written as an *apologia* for Paul in view of the impending trial. Romans come out of it well, the stress is always on Christianity as a *lawful religion,* connected with Judaism which Rome recognized, and in no way a socially or politically disruptive force.

cost. Whether or not Paul had in mind the Roman *res publica* in thinking of the Church, the *ekklesia*, it was fitting that a Roman citizen had the decisive share in the forward movement.

Paul the Greek

But Paul was also a Greek, by which we mean that he lived in a Greek-speaking, Greek-thinking and Greek-living world. The language of that world, in which Paul spoke and wrote (and possibly thought, though his first language was Aramaic) was the lively *koine* or "common" Greek, well known to us from the papyri discoveries of the last century as well as from the New Testament; a kind of colloquial Greek suited to all classes from Corinthian stevedores to Roman courtiers. Paul was at home in the great "Greek" cities of the Empire—Tarsus, Antioch, Ephesus, Corinth—and showed on the occasion of a memorable visit to Athens that his mind could adapt itself to Greek philosophy and that he could quote Stoic poets off the cuff when the chance came his way (Acts 17:28). It might not seem fashionable to add that there is about Paul something of the citizen of the Greek *polis* (city-state) of the classical Athenian period—in particular as regards that inalienable right to get up and say what you think needs saying without fear of being shut up by some petty tyrant— what the Greeks call *parresia*—"the right to say everything." This right, incidentally, Paul builds into his picture of life in the Christian society. His initiation into this kind of life no doubt began with his earliest days in Tarsus, then a great city with a university and, of course, gymnasia, theater, art schools, stadium and the rest. All this makes quite different reading, when we come to the letters, from what we find in the Gospels with their predominantly country metaphors and ways of speaking. Paul draws his metaphors from the city—military life, slavery, sport, the municipal guilds and the like.[4] Moreover Tarsus, besides being one of the largest cities in the Empire—after Rome, Alexandria, Antioch and Ephesus—was also an international port and situated at a crucial point on the land route from the East to the Roman province of Asia (with its capital Ephesus) and Europe—just below the gap in the Taurus mountains where the railway now goes through at Pozanti, then known as the Cilician Gates. It is therefore easy to see it as a cosmopolitan city and Paul as familiar from his earliest years with all manner of people from every part of the world.

Paul the Jew

But we have to be careful here. *Paul was also a Jew,* son of Pharisees and destined for the rabbinate. He would therefore have looked out at that world, upon which he was to pronounce the terrible indictment we find in the first chapter of Romans, with the eyes of a Jew and a devout member of the Tarsus ghetto com-

---

[4] I Corinthians 9:24–27 suggests Paul may have taken a day off to watch the Isthmian Games (they were celebrated every second year); he uses terms connected with sprinting and boxing—words like *adokimos*—disqualified, *hypopiazo*—hit below the eyes. At the end, looking back over his life, he sees it as an athletic contest, a race, and he has now broken the tape (2 Timothy 4:7). Whether or not he had ever seen the games in the great amphitheater at Ephesus which held over 20,000, he speaks to the Corinthians, metaphorically, of having "fought with beasts" in that city (I Corinthians 15:32) and represents their fight against the supernatural enemy in terms of gladiatorial combat (Ephesians 6:10–17).

munity. He speaks more than once in his letters, and with pride, of his Jewish upbringing—he was "a Hebrew born of Hebrews" (Philippians 3:5), member of the tribe of Benjamin (his namesake, Saul the king, was too), probably with connections in the "old country."[5] His being destined for the rabbinate would have implied a preparation something like that for the priesthood at the present day, except considerably more strict. Like the Jewish children one can still see in the orthodox section of the new city of Jerusalem, with their long side curls and skull caps, he would have played few games, spent long hours in the synagogue school under the direction of the *hazzan* learning the scriptures by rote (he quotes them, often by memory, about two hundred times in his letters) and would have worshiped in the synagogue with the adults from the age of thirteen, wearing his *tallith* or prayer-shawl. *Of the three aspects we mentioned, this is certainly the decisive one in Paul's early years and therefore for the rest of his life,* and even reading his letters to Christian Churches we shall misunderstand him if we forget for long that we are dealing with a convert rabbi. No doubt for many Christians today, to a great extent due to ignorance, the world in which Paul was brought up is a strange and perhaps even repellent one. But Paul remained to the end passionately attached to his people, to that strange world which defied history (and continues to do so):

> I could wish that I myself were accursed and cut off from Christ for the sake of my brethren, my kinsmen by race. They are Israelites, and to them belong the sonship, the glory, the covenants, the

[5] St. Jerome tells us that his family came from Gischala in Galilee.

giving of the Law, the worship and the promises;
to them belong the patriarchs, and of their race,
according to the flesh, is the Christ.

(Romans 9:3–5)

After the first or primary stage of his education at
Tarsus, at an age when his contemporaries of equal
social and intellectual standing were applying for ad-
mission to the university of their native city, Paul was
packed off to Jerusalem to continue his religious studies
under the greatest master of that time, Gamaliel the
Elder, who himself makes a brief appearance in Luke's
story, urging moderation on the Jewish supreme council
bent on eradicating the early Christian movement (Acts
5:34–40). Paul probably stayed with his sister who
married into a highly ranked Jerusalem family (Acts
23:16), and no doubt worshiped at the synagogue of
his native Cilicia which we have already mentioned.
*There can be no doubt about his being a hundred per-
cent Jew and Pharisee at this period;* later on he tells us
himself: "I advanced in Judaism beyond many of my
own age among my people, so extremely zealous was I
for the traditions of my fathers" (Galatians 1:14).

This statement is borne out by his attitude to the
new movement which had sprung up within Palestinian
Judaism and which must have seemed to Paul not just a
"heresy" (Acts 24:14) but something blasphemous and
destructive of everything he had been brought up to
believe in. Luke tells us that the lynching of Stephen
triggered a widespread persecution against the Hellenistic element in the early community (the apostles,
curiously enough, were left in peace, Acts 8:1) and
that Saul laid waste the Church, proscribing, imprison-
ing, executing, with the result—providential as it hap-

pened—that these ardent Christian missionaries of the first hour moved north into cities like Damascus and Antioch, eventually setting up the first great missionary center of the Church's history in the latter city. Paul decided to follow them and, after obtaining letters of introduction from the Jerusalem high priest to the leader of the Damascus synagogue, set off in pursuit.

Part II
Personal Encounter

ON the road, however, something extraordinary happened, an experience so violent and traumatic that when he did finally arrive in the city he was blind and neither ate nor drank for three days.

Luke's history contains altogether three accounts of what took place, which gives us some idea of the importance he—and Paul—attached to it: once as part of the straightforward history (chapter 9), once in the exciting account of Paul's last-ditch defense before a crowd after his blood, standing on the steps of the Roman barracks in Jerusalem (chapter 22), a third time in the relative calm of the audience hall at Caesarea in the presence of King Herod Agrippa (chapter 26). The small divergences which we detect in reading these accounts consecutively are only what we would expect, seeing that the speeches, which in any case were not tape-recorded, were pronounced more than twenty years after the event and Acts itself written more than thirty years after. There was the literally blinding light, the voice, Paul's bewildered question and the order to go on into the city and await developments. History records other tremendous personal experiences of this kind, and it is always difficult for the person concerned to give a rational account of what happened afterwards. The same for Paul; but *what is important is the complete change, and the profound influence which it continued to have on him for the rest of his life.*

There has been a tremendous crop of speculation about what really took place in this "conversion." Everything has been tried: brain fag, sunstroke, the strain of a long journey, epilepsy, lightning or a thunderbolt. It has even been suggested (by a nine-teenth-century scholar called Gottlieb Paulus) that it was just a way of saying that Paul actually met Jesus who had in fact recovered after having been taken down from the cross. Anyone who has read George Moore's novel *The Brook Kerith,* or Robert Grave's *Jesus in Rome* will have some idea of this approach, and it will suffice here to say that no genuine scholar takes it seriously. It is quite a different question to ask whether this event, so utterly sudden and unexpected as it appears to have been, was prepared for in any way. We cannot exclude the possibility that Paul may have seen Jesus on a previous visit to Jerusalem, perhaps on one of the pilgrim feasts, or that he may even have arrived before the crucifixion. He may have experienced doubts about the rightness of his action—the voice in the vision spoke of "kicking against the goad" (Acts 26:14)—since he must surely have known of the prudent attitude of his master Gamaliel with regard to the new movement (Acts 5:34–39), and the danger that in opposing it he was opposing God. Doubts may also have been sown by Stephen's line of argument—which is similar to that taken up later by Paul himself[1] —and we might add that if, as is likely, his journey north took him along the old trade route through Galilee, the memory of the crucified carpenter could have been brought vividly to his mind and, in fact, his

---

[1] Thus we should not forget that Paul was not the first to break with Judaism; in this, as in his missionary activity in general, he fits into the Hellenistic Christian effort.

"revelation"—for that is what he himself calls it (Galatians 1:12)—took place in the same Decapolis, the region of the Ten Cities of which Damascus was one, in which the messianic identity of Jesus was "revealed" to Peter (see Matthew 16:17).

Speculations based on some trends in modern psychological research applied to a more or less questionable reconstruction of Paul's early life—all with a view to "getting inside" the experience on the Damascus road—have to be taken with a good pinch of salt. Thus, it is risky to start from passages in his letters which *look* autobiographical, such as the famous one on the moral helplessness of man faced with the demands of God's law concluding with the cry: "Wretched man that I am! Who will deliver me from this body of death?" (Romans 7:7–24)—and then to go on to speak of the inevitable consequences of a long suppression of the libido. At the same time, the constant attempt to observe in all its details a legalistic religion like Pharisaism—not only the Old Testament Law (in which Pharisees of Paul's day distinguished more than six hundred different precepts) but also the traditions, of the kind we constantly encounter in the Gospels— must have taken its toll right up to the time of his conversion, and it is well known how a period of suppression, either guilty or otherwise, can end in a kind of explosion of the subconscious which brings what is under the surface into the full light of consciousness. Paul always understood his revelation as absolutely supernatural, directly, vertically from God, making him an apostle; but there is no reason to deny that it could have been prepared, within God's providence, by the whole history of his life up till then.

It is more important, however, to note what it

meant to Paul in view of the future. It was *God reveal-
ing his Son in him* (see Galatians 1:12 and I Corinthians 9:1) and, as such, a complete break with the past.
Referring to it later on, writing to the community at
Philippi, he speaks of his early life as a Jew, his high
standing, the progress he had made, and goes on: "I
count everything as loss because of the surpassing worth
of knowing Christ Jesus my Lord" (Philippians 3:8).
The past disappeared and from that moment he was *in
Christ* and "if anyone is in Christ he is a new creation"
(II Corinthians 5:17). *It was also, we must remember,
the last of the appearances of the risen Lord:*

He appeared to Cephas, then to the twelve.
Then he appeared to more than five hundred brethren at
    one time most of whom are still alive . . .
Then he appeared to James, then to all the apostles.
Last of all, as to one untimely born, he appeared also
    to me.   (I Corinthians 15:5–8).

This is an important point since it made him an apostle
like the Twelve and authenticated his mission in the
face of the many who did not readily accept the
credentials of this ex-Pharisee.

Upon his arrival at Damascus he was led, still half
insensible and unseeing, through the noisy bazaars of
that ancient city to the house of a Jewish contact called
Judas who lived on Straight Street.[2] How long he
remained there with his presumably still dazed retinue
we are not told; but he was visited by a member of the

---

[2] The street is still there, but is only a shadow of what it
must have been in Paul's day. The pilgrim or tourist who is
willing to suspend his critical faculties can also see St. Paul's
Window from which he was lowered, the House of St. Ananias
and the spot where Paul was baptized.

Christian community, which had already been established there, a certain Ananias who had the gift of healing which was often exercised in the early Christian communities, who gave him back his sight and baptized him, no doubt after a short period of instruction. Soon he was going the rounds of the synagogues pleading the cause of the despised group which he had come to stamp out. The story of how, at this point, he made the first of several last-minute escapes from death is well known (Acts 9:23–25; II Corinthians 11:32–33). He went into hiding in some desert spot south of the city—Damascus was an important center of the Nabataean Arab kingdom of Aretas IV—which provided him with the chance of thinking over his past life in the light of the tremendous experience which he had had and of rereading and remeditating the scriptures in the light of the Christ-event. After some time he was able to return to the city where he remained as a missionary for the next three years.

Part III
What Did Christ Mean to Paul?

A NYONE who wants to understand Paul — even the uncommitted historian who acknowledges the enormous influence which he has exercised on the history of the last one thousand nine hundred years— has to start by asking that question. All the more so the Christian for whom his faith is a reality; he must ask it not in the spirit of a revivalist meeting which leaves one either amused or embarrassed, but soberly and objectively. It may mean putting out of our minds for the moment some rather second-class examples of religious art and some overemotional sermons we may have heard. Paul's kind of concern goes far beyond this level. "For me," he wrote to the Christians of Philippi, "to be alive means Christ." What did he mean?

We might begin by saying what he did not mean. *One thing that strikes the first-time reader of Paul's letters is that they give us so few facts or details about the life of Christ*. It would be too bad if we had to reconstruct that life on the basis of what we find there. He tells us that Jesus was of David's race (Romans 1:3), mentions his being born of a woman, though he does not follow this up as the later apocryphal writings do (Galatians 4:4). Nothing about his family, the public ministry, no harrowing details about the passion; hardly anything, in short, outside of the mere "event" of death-resurrection and the celebration of the death in the eucharistic meal (I Corinthians 11). There are references to Christ's teaching necessary for the moral formation of his Christians; and he actually gives us a saying which we do not find in the Gospels.[1] He sums it up by stating quite plainly that he is not interested in knowing Christ "from a human point of view" (II Corinthians 5:16).

Why this distressing lack of interest in the life of Jesus which we find in Paul and the early Christians in general? The reason is surely that *they were so overwhelmed by the presentness of Christ with them in their life together in community, experienced in a direct and powerful way* as will be evident to anyone reading Acts, that this just did not occur to them. Others had known the Lord in the flesh and blood (". . . that which we have seen with our eyes, which we have looked at and touched with our hands . . ." (I John 1:1); but for Paul, after his experience, and for his Christians, he was present "in spirit." This was not just in the rather vague way in which we speak of a dead person's spirit living on after him. When Peter had to find a way of explaining what had happened at the first Pentecost, he quoted from one of the prophets a passage about the "pouring out of the Spirit" in the last age, and it is the Spirit which makes Christ present to the Church and to each Christian, a presence which is, however, impossible to the person who chooses to remain on the purely natural level. For Paul, too, this new presence is made possible through the risen Christ, since for him "the Lord is the Spirit" (II Corinthians 3:18).

There is another aspect to this. Paul and his Christians did not think of the resurrection as a past event which continued to influence their lives; they saw them-

---

[1] "It is more blessed to give than to receive" (Acts 20:35).

selves as living *within* an event which began with the resurrection but which had yet to be completed in the coming of the risen Lord in a future which for many of them must have seemed imminent. This total event is divided up for us in the Creed: "crucified, dead and buried . . . descended into hell . . . the third day rose again from the dead . . . ascended into heaven . . . from thence he shall come," but for the first Christians these were different stages in the one final intervention of God in history by which he has chosen to bring the whole process to perfection in "the fullness of time."

When we think of this it is easy to see why the early Church did not show so much interest in the material details of the thirty-five to forty years that Jesus lived on this earth. We might feel sorry about this, and have thoughts about what would have happened if he had lived in our day, with television, tape recorders, photography . . . perhaps the visit of Pope Paul VI to Palestine might give us some vague and remote idea. Of course, the supposition is not well-founded since realization always comes too late—as it did for so many of the contemporaries of Jesus in the first century. At any rate, the writing up of "all that Jesus began to do and to teach" was undertaken thoroughly only when the prospect of an immediate return in glory paled with the passing of time, in particular after the fall of Jerusalem (A.D. 70). In reading the four Gospels we have always to bear in mind that gap of thirty years or so between the death of the Lord and their composition.

What *was* of vital interest to the apostolic community of Jerusalem, to Stephen and the Hellenistic missionaries and to Paul, was *spreading the oral Gospel, the "good news of God," namely, how God had brought his promises, of which the scriptures speak, to comple-*

tion in the death and resurrection of Jesus. Notice how
Ananias, in explaining the meaning of Paul's apparition,
to him in Damascus, says: "The God of our fathers
appointed you to know his will" (Acts 22:14). It was
the same God of the fathers who had raised Jesus from
the dead: "The God of Abraham and of Isaac and of
Jacob, the God of our fathers, glorified his servant Jesus
whom you delivered up . . . whom God raised from the
dead" (Acts 3:13–15). For these men the scriptures
by which they had lived all their lives, the psalms they
had recited in the synagogue, suddenly came alive.
Given this final event they made sense; without it they
continued to be a dark puzzle:

> To this day (says Paul speaking of the Jews),
> when they read the Old Testament, the same veil
> remains unlifted because only through Christ is it
> taken away. Yes, to this day, whenever Moses is
> read, a veil lies over their minds; but when a man
> turns to the Lord the veil is removed.
>
> (II Corinthians 3:14–16)

*This means that sacred history, the history of salvation,
the working of God throughout time and space, had
come to completion in the event to which the apostolic
community witnessed.* This is what Luke is saying when
he speaks of the different nationalities at Pentecost
hearing proclaimed "the mighty works of God" (Acts
2:11). This means also that Paul's understanding of
Christ must have begun with the scriptures, that his
experience must have given sense and coherence to
what he already knew. This obliges us to follow the
same line in our attempt to understand and then to live
the central *fact* of our faith. It might be well, therefore,
to trace out roughly the main lines of this understanding

of Christ in the first years of the Church's history and to draw some conclusions.

In order to do this we might take a closer look at Peter's address to the Roman centurion and his family and retainers, which we find in Luke's history of the early Church, the Acts of the Apostles. This took place only a few years after the crucifixion in the town of Caesarea on the Mediterranean coast which was the Roman headquarters in Palestine. Since for Peter this was the first pagan, that is, non-Jewish family to be converted, the event must have had a special significance for him and this can in fact be inferred from the way he spoke. The address should be read carefully (see Acts 10:34–43) with the assistance of the following summary.[2]

34–35   The whole object of life is *to be acceptable to God* ("acceptable" is really a liturgical term used of a sacrifice which God could accept, e.g. the sacrifice of Abel or Melchizedek). Following Christ in the Christian life is offered as a way of reaching this goal, as in fact *the* way, since it is the way offered positively by God himself, not thought out by man. This prepares for what follows.

36   The Christian message is *the Word* sent by God to Israel and then to the whole world; it is *the good news* which God gives through Jesus Christ.

37   A summary of the good news (i.e. the Gospel) follows. The general outline had already been fixed by constant repetition: ministry of John

---

[2] Only one example is given in the text. For other summaries see pp. 123ff.

the Baptist—public ministry in Galilee—in Judea.

38 Summarized from a different angle: the *anointing with the Holy Spirit and with power* refers doubtless to the baptism of Jesus as the inauguration of his public ministry, while the word "power" suggests the miracles (in the Synoptic Gospels the word "power," *dynamis,* is the word used for "miracle"). This is completed by the reference to the healings and exorcisms which form such a great part of the written Gospels.

39–40 Leads up to the last phase—in Jerusalem. The climax is *one* event which has two sides: *they* put him to death; but *God* raised him on the third day and made him manifest. Death and resurrection are somehow part of the one event, the climax of all salvation history.

41 The reality of the resurrection is emphasized by the fact that they *ate and drank* with him. Hence the great importance attached to witnesses of the resurrection, though there is no list given as is usual at this point in the summaries.

42 The coming of Christ to judge the world as the last stage of the great event of redemption which begins with the crucifixion. We should note that God is still the subject of the whole action—he sends the good news (36), he is with Jesus (38), he raised him from the dead (40) and chose witnesses to the resurrection (41) and he finally appoints Christ as universal judge (42).

43 We are invited (with Cornelius) to answer this invitation by faith, that is, commitment of our

lives, which brings with it the forgiveness of
our sins.

We might note, in addition, two discourses of Paul
to pagan listeners: the first to a peasant audience at
Konya (Acts 14:15–17). There is no bible history as
in the case we have considered—it would have meant
nothing to them—but this is implied in the "good news"
which is the call to turn away from idols to serve "the
living God," that is, the God who is manifest in nature
and in history. For converts with this background,
sacred history as such would have to come at a later
stage. The second is the address on Mars' Hill in
Athens to a philosophical audience in which again Paul
seeks a common denominator, in this case religious
sentiment. Here again, it is not sacred history but a
preparation for it, by showing how natural man, the
ideal of Greek civilization at its best, does not achieve
perfection by himself, but rather falls under the judg-
ment of God which will be carried out by "a man"
whom God has raised from the dead. At this point they
stopped listening.

From this brief scheme, helped out by the other
New Testament summaries, we can easily deduce the
basic structure of the Christian message and therefore
of Paul's message. Sacred history is a continuous historical process set in motion by the promise which God
made to Abraham and culminating in the "good news"
that God had fulfilled this promise in the resurrection
of Jesus. This last, however, implied certain facts about
Jesus which we find here, and which were later filled out
into the written Gospels. Thus, it is not difficult to see
how the original pattern: John the Baptist; baptism of
Jesus; ministry in Galilee, Judaea, Jerusalem; passion,

death, burial and rising from the dead, which we find here in the original Jerusalem message and partially in that of Paul, was filled out by Mark the "interpreter" of Peter in his Gospel and how all the Gospels are dominated and dictated by the resurrection and were, so to speak, written backwards from this point. The resurrection implies the passion (they are really two "moments" of the same event) written to explain *why* rather than *how* Christ died—which has led one scholar to define a Gospel as a passion narrative with a long introduction (of 688 verses in Mark, 253, more than a third, deal with the last week in the life of Christ). All through the Gospels, finally, the link with the Old Testament is kept unbroken since Gospel is good news and the news is, according to Mark's version, that "the time (of fulfilment) is at hand."

This is the Gospel Paul received, passed on, and was commissioned by the risen Lord to proclaim to all nations. We can begin to answer the question which stands at the head of this section only within this context. Perhaps it will clarify the issues implied in the question if we state the meaning of Christ for Paul in four propositions:

1. The risen Christ is the climax of salvation history

2. The risen Christ is God for us

3. Christianity is not a religion but a Person and an Event

4. God comes to us through Christ only in the Church.

A brief note on each will not be out of place at this stage leaving further development to a later section.

1. *The Risen Christ Is the Climax of Salvation History*

Paul's vision led him to rethink the whole of his past life, his reading of the scriptures, his view of the world and of history. The bottom had suddenly fallen out of his life, up till that time based on the full observance of the Torah, the Jewish Law. From then onward the revelation of the risen Lord holds the center. This process, however, took a whole lifetime and we can trace its main stages in Acts and in the correspondence.

A. In the first stage, roughly down to the so-called "Council of Jerusalem" and the bitter struggle with the Judaeo-Christian element, Paul's presentation of the story of God's action in history, aiming to show how he fulfills the promises made to the holy men of the Old Testament period in Jesus, is identical with that of the Jerusalem apostolic community. This can be seen by glancing at the scheme of his synagogue sermon at Antioch in Pisidia (p. 125) and fits in with what he himself tells us about his visit to the leaders of the Jerusalem Church in order to "check" "the Gospel which I preach among the Gentiles, lest somehow I should be running or had run in vain" (Galatians 2:2). This is important in showing us that there is no such thing as a "Pauline" doctrine apart from that of the Church and no real dispute, as was long supposed, between Paul and the primitive Church in Jerusalem.

B. The second stage corresponds with the first letters written by Paul which have survived. Most of Paul's letters had the object of keeping in touch with the communities he had set up, and while dealing to a great extent with the solution of everyday difficulties experienced by these communities, they give us a good guide to how his thinking about Christ and the Christ-event developed. Probably the earliest were the two short letters, which we call I and II Thessalonians, written to the newly-founded Christian community at Salonika. Since this Church was, however, predominantly non-Jewish, there is little Old Testament history; in fact we find here the same approach as we have seen in Acts 14 with a pagan, peasant audience—beginning with the turning from idols to serve the living God, then the simple story of Jesus' death and resurrection. When, however, we turn to Galatians, written probably a couple of years later, we soon realize something has gone wrong. Instead of the usual warm opening phrases, he begins with a blunt negative and goes on at once to express not his thanksgiving, as is usual, but his astonishment. He is angry with a group of people who had "slipped in to spy out our freedom which we have in Christ Jesus" (Galatians 2:4), whom later he does not hesitate to call "dogs" and "evil workers" (Philippians 3:2). These were the Judaeo-Christians who were teaching, in effect, that one had to be a Jew first and only then a Christian or, which comes to the same thing, that circumcision was a necessary condition for entering the Christian Church. This was a vital point since it implied that Christianity was to be a branch of Judaism and therefore not really a universal faith, and it led Paul to a vigorous reinterpretation of Old Testament history, somewhat along the lines of Stephen and the Hellenists.

His point is, briefly, that Judaism as a religious system has been canceled by what God has done in Christ. The pivotal point in the argument is Abraham to whom, in a strong and original phrase, the Gospel was preached in advance (Galatians 3:8), meaning that the promise which God made to this Aramaean sheik (Genesis 12:3) is fulfilled in its definitive form in the death and resurrection of Jesus. Since both circumcision and the Law were given later than this promise—in the latter case 430 years later (Galatians 3:17)—they play only a secondary role. Here (and elsewhere) Paul says something which must have seemed the ultimate in blasphemy to his one-time fellow-religionists, namely, that the real purpose of the Law was to show up man's moral helplessness (since it was never really observed) and therefore the need for something of a higher order (Galatians 3:19–22; cf. also I Corinthians 15:56). The whole of the old order is pictured as a tutor or trustee for mankind during its minority; but the whole purpose of education, as both teachers and those taught will certainly agree, is that as soon as possible it may be dispensed with. And so Christianity is *mankind's coming of age*—the entering into the freedom of the children of God (Galatians 4:1–7). The old order dies with Christ on the cross (6:14).

The conclusion, therefore, is that Christ is indeed the climax of salvation history—and of all history—as supposed also in the early sermons in Acts; *but this climax transcends the whole of this history, that is, goes beyond it and is the beginning of something absolutely new.* Not only is it founded in a new covenant or alliance (I Corinthians 11:25), Christ is the new Adam, the first of the new race (Romans 5:12; I Corinthians 15:45) and the man that is "in Christ" is a "new creation" (II Corinthians 5:17; Galatians 6:15). This insight we owe to Paul.

C. Many of these eruptive and disruptive ideas reappear and are further developed and clarified in the letters to Corinth and Rome written towards the end of the fifth decade. We recall that Luke's story ends with the beginning of Paul's imprisonment (house arrest might be a more apt description) in Rome awaiting trial. During this enforced confinement of two years at Nero's pleasure, Paul had time to think over his tremendous experiences and work out some of the consequences. We find something of this process in the letters he dictated during this period to the communities at Philippi in Macedonia and those in the Roman province of Asia (Ephesians, Colossians).

Reading these magnificent statements of faith we note how the Jewish, Old Testament perspective has almost disappeared; Christ is the end, the goal, of a whole vast process of movement and transformation within nature and of the long history of mankind from creation down to the present moment. In him, "the first-born from the dead," God's plan[3], the mystery hidden from ages (Colossians 1:26), is completed. This comprehensive plan of God, stretching through all time, includes first of all mankind, *us*—"God chose us in him from the foundation of the world" (Ephesians 1:4)— but also the whole of the universe with its long history —"a plan for the fullness of time, to unite all things in him, things in heaven and things on earth" (Ephesians 1:10). This forward movement can be satisfactorily explained, according to Paul, only from the end, the goal—the risen Lord who appeared to him on the Damascus road:

[3] The Greek word is *oikonomia* which means an ordered whole and is a key word for the history of salvation.

He is the image of the invisible God, the first-
born of all creation; for in him all things were created in heaven and on earth, visible and invisible
. . . all things were created through him and for
him. He is before all things and in him all things
hold together. He is the head of the body, the
Church; he is the beginning, the firstborn from
the dead, that in everything he might be preemi-
nent. For in him all the fullness of God was pleased
to dwell, and through him to reconcile to himself
all things, whether on earth or in heaven, making
peace by the blood of his cross.

(Colossians 1:15–20)

2. *The Risen Christ Is God for Us*

We may have noticed, in reading the New Testament summaries on page 123, something rather dis-
concerting. The public ministry is described as "mighty
works and wonders and signs *which God did through
him";* God "raises" Jesus from the dead—in fact
hardly ever in the New Testament does Jesus "rise"
from the dead—and he does not "ascend" but is
"taken up" into heaven (thus we should speak, as Luke
in fact does in his Gospel (9:51), of an *assumption*
rather than an *ascension*). Later on, in describing the
work of redemption, Paul will say: "God was recon-
ciling the world to himself *through Christ"* (II Corinthians 5:19).

In order to explain this, we have to bear in mind
that biblical revelation is different from any other
religious system that we know of, in that while the
latter deals with man striving for union with a god, the
bible speaks to us of God coming to man. Here, it is
God who acts, who takes the initiative. No other religious document we know is so realistic about sin and

man's moral helplessness; and yet we note how God stays with the sinner and how the forward line continues in spite of sin. Thus, he clothes the first couple after their sin, he protects Cain from the consequences of his crime, he forgives David and gives him a son for the one who had died. In the different literary strands in the Old Testament, which are studied in other books of this series, he is represented in different ways as *the God who is near* and who has committed himself to complete what he has already initiated in the Alliance. On Sinai, in the Torah, he revealed himself as Will, but will is a function of personality and cannot exist, so to speak, up in the air. The Christ-event, therefore, is the point at which this same God reveals himself completely as person, the point at which he comes to us in the fullest possible way.

After centuries of controversy, especially the long debate with the followers of Arius in the third and fourth centuries,[4] we now have a precise terminology to express the relationship of the Jesus of the Gospels to the divinity, and to avoid the kind of misinterpretation which was so common in the early centuries. The creeds state that Jesus "rose from the dead," "ascended into heaven." But, as we have seen, the way the New Testament speaks of these matters shows us that Jesus is not just a divine person as a sort of static element in the Trinity; the relationship is dynamic not static, for in him through the Spirit, God communicates to us his own life which we are invited to share as adopted sons with Christ the firstborn, the image, of God.

[4] Arianism, which threatened to swamp the whole Church in this period, held that the Son was not of identical nature with the Father; he was therefore a man even if a very extraordinary man, "a Christian saint" as Newman put it.

3. *Christianity Is Not a Religion but a Person and an Event*

The first followers of Jesus, after the resurrection, continued saying the same prayers (the psalms), frequenting the Temple, observing Jewish food laws and the rest—Jews practicing the Jewish faith. They realized that the event to which they testified and on the real historical truth of which they staked everything had fulfilled the old order, but they still saw this fulfillment *within* the old order—that is, as the culmination of Judaism.

It was only among the hard knocks of experience and in particular in the struggle with the extreme Judaic element in the early Church that Christians began to realize their real identity, their uniqueness. It is interesting in this respect to see how the new movement was identified and classified by others in this early period and how early Christians describe themselves. Tertullus, spokesman for the Jews accusing Paul in Jerusalem, refers to him as "a ringleader of the sect of the Nazarenes" (Acts 24:5)—meaning a heresy from official Judaism—a designation which Paul in his answer rejects. So, too, the Jewish delegation which meets Paul on his arrival in Rome (Acts 28:22). For the official Roman world, little interested in religions apart from their political implications, the Christian movement was indistinguishable from the Jewish "religion"—or "superstition" as the word is often translated.[5] This

---

[5] In Pliny's letter to Trajan about A.D. 110 Christianity, as practiced in Bithynia, the province of which he was proconsul, was "a base and degrading superstition"; for Tacitus, writing just a few years later, it was a "detestable superstition," one of the many base oriental cults that found their way to Rome "where all atrocious and shameful things come together and are celebrated."

comes through clearly in Festus' laconic presentation of Paul's case to king Agrippa: "They (i.e. his Jewish accusers) had certain points of dispute with him about their own superstition and about one Jesus who was dead but whom Paul asserted to be alive" (Acts 25:19).

It is significant, though, that the early Christians do not accept this description with its implication that they are just a Jewish splinter group. They never think of themselves either as a new religion supplanting the old, or as a "system," but as a group of people called by God to witness to a tremendous experience and to live that experience in their own lives and, as far as possible, transmit it to others. They refer to themselves mostly as "The Way" which reminds us of Jesus' words: "I am the Way," recorded by John.

It was Paul's great contribution to have worked this truth out ruthlessly to its logical conclusions and not just in theory but in the arena of everyday life. It would take another book to show in detail and illustrate how he worked out the principle that Judaism was superseded for the Christian—circumcision, the integral observance of the Torah, food laws, the sacrificial system, all gave way to the new reality in Christ. He reacted violently to any attempt at going back to what they had left behind. There is, as Paul knew well, a recurring tendency in our human nature to fall back on routine, on fixed form, seeking security both religious and intellectual in just going through the paces without trying to think through to the meaning of what we are doing—if it has any. "Why do you submit to regulations?" he snaps at the Colossians. "Do not handle! Do not taste! Do not touch!" "You observe days and months and seasons and years!" he says to the Galatians in despair, "I am afraid I have labored over you in vain." Already, in such a short time, they had turned that tremendous hope, that *Presence,* into a "religion" of the Tibetan prayer-wheel type.

In a real sense, therefore, the fact that Judaism was superseded meant that *religion as such* was, since all the religious movements of history find their answer in Christ on the cross, Christ risen from the dead. Therefore being a Christian for Paul did not mean professing a religion in the dictionary sense of "a system of faith and worship," but realizing the cross and the new, risen life of Christ in one's own life. How this was to be done we shall see at a later stage.

4. *God Comes to Us through Christ Only in the Church*

It might have escaped us in reading the accounts of Paul's conversion that the voice said to him: "I am Jesus whom you are persecuting," implying the identity of Jesus and the Church; also that he was not given a private revelation of hidden truths, as we might expect from similar incidents in other religions, but was put in touch with a member of the Damascus Christian community who cured, instructed and baptized him. Community, belonging together, mutual interdependence is essential to the Christian life.

It is a fact that God's call, even when made to individuals, is always in view of the group, the community. Abraham is called, but only in view of the blessing intended for his descendants; the Exodus, the pivot and fulcrum of Old Testament revelation, is a social experience resulting in the creation of a sacred community; the kings are important only as representatives of the people, since they have no destiny and no place in God's scheme apart from the destiny of the people of god. *The* theme of the prophetic books is that of the identity and survival of that people, which is *not* identical with historical Israel as such, the nation with its king, since God's call went out before the nation came into existence, and when it finally came to fulfillment the nation as such had ceased to exist. God calls a person, therefore, out of the world and into his sacred community.

We might feel like objecting at this point—with very many others at the present day — Why can't I just set up my own private understanding with God? Why should the Christian Church make such a peremptory claim on my attention to the exclusion of any other possibility? We have to be careful in answering this very reasonable objection. "Signed up" membership in the Church is not always necessary for achieving the object of life, which is reconciliation with God; else what of the millions of good living pagans in the world today who have no remote hope of receiving baptism? At the same time, no one can go to God except through Christ, which implies that there must exist a hidden order of grace, a hidden contact with Christ and the Church by which the good Buddhist, Taoist or Mohammedan is saved—or even the good person who belongs to no organized faith. The situation of these people can be compared to that of those outside the boundaries of God's people in the old order before Christ. Even within the rather narrow-minded and exclusive Jewish community of the Exile and after, this idea began to penetrate—"Shall I not pity Nineveh in which there are more than a hundred and twenty thousand persons who do not know their right hand from their left? (Jonah 4:11).

God's call to enter the Church does not, then, come to all, but when it comes it must be accepted—with faith, without questioning, even when no guarantees are given; that is why Abraham is the ideal of all true believers. Faith means, first and foremost, saying "Yes" to God's invitation. The fact is that God's plan, the mystery in the sense explained above, can be fulfilled only through a community. Isolated individuals cannot throw any effective weight against the gravitational force of sin in the world, even when serving God according to their lights. Moreover, and this is the decisive answer, the Church is *for* the world; it is God's way of working out the destiny of mankind and of all creation which depends upon mankind.[6] That is what Paul means when he speaks of making all men see "what is the plan of the mystery hidden for ages in God who created all things; that *through the Church* the manifold wisdom of God might now be made known" (in Ephesians 3:9–10). We cooperate with this design whether we like it or not or even whether we think of it or not; but God has invited us Christians to do so freely, as free citizens of the divine commonwealth.

There is a feeling abroad in our day, even more so than in Paul's, of the desirability and even necessity of unity and convergence in mankind. This movement toward unity has to overcome barriers at different levels: nationalism, social class distinction, racialism and the like by finding the common element, the fundamental human element which unites men together. It is at this level that the Church works, and we Christians believe that it is only through the Church that this unity,

[6] Adrian Hastings, *The Church's No. 1 Problem: Mission,* in the series, *Where We Stand.*

which is fundamentally moral in character, can be accomplished, for all who are baptized members of the Church share the common dignity of children of God:

> In Christ Jesus you are all sons of God by faith, for as many of you as have been baptized into Christ have put on Christ. There is neither Jew nor Greek, there is neither slave nor free, there is neither male nor female; for you are all one in Christ Jesus. (Galatians 3:26–28)

Part IV
Taking the Gospel to the World

WHEN we hear the word "missionary" we are apt to think of an affable clerical gentleman, bearded and wearing a white cassock, surrounded by numerous black children. Mission countries are all far distant, certainly outside of Europe, and missionaries have to be supported by collecting money. Yet the first missionary center was directed by a group of five, two of whom were Africans; the first missionaries to evangelize Europe came from Asia; and the first missions collected for the "home country"—for the Christian communities in Jerusalem and Judaea!

The First Missionary Center

The fact is that our popular idea belongs properly to the colonial epoch and is now out of date. Then, missionaries together with trade followed the flag—and of course did a great work of evangelization and civilization even if, in some cases, their work did not bear fruit in the long run owing to faulty method. Now we use terms such as *La Mission de France* which show a more realistic appraisal of the situation—indeed we could with equal right speak also of the *English Mission* as our forebears did in the sixteenth century.

Paul, who was one of the first missionaries to Europe, saw missionary activity, in the strict sense of the word, as an essential of the Christian life, not just as

an extra. The revelation of Christ in him gave him his
mission at the same time it led him to baptism; in fact,
the word "apostle" is simply Greek for missionary
(*apostello*—"I send on a mission") and all Christians
share in the mandate given by the risen Christ: "Go,
therefore, and make disciples of all nations." This does
not imply that all Christians have to be missionaries in
the more specialized sense in which Paul and Barnabas
were, or the 60,000 or so missionary priests and brothers and an unspecified number of lay missionaries are
at the present day; but he saw baptism as implying the
presence of the Christian in and to the world, bringing
Christ to it by the moral force of the Christian life and
witness of the convinced believer. There was no such
thing as a static Christian for Paul, since he conceived
Christianity in organic terms, and there is no such thing
as a static organism. His own missionary career is the
best illustration of the theory, and to this career we now
turn.

We should state at once that what follows is not
meant to be an exhaustive commentary on Acts, much
less a substitute for a reading of the second half of this
fascinating composition. Doubtful and disputed questions—such as Luke's chronology and literary methods
—could not be gone into, and the adoption of one
theory to the apparent exclusion of other possibilities
is often dictated by purely practical considerations. Our
purpose is to keep our eye on Paul and try to deduce
from the activity the inner motivating forces from which
it sprang in order to be able to draw, at a later stage,
some conclusions of permanent value for our understanding of the Christian life.

The usual division into three missionary journeys
is, to begin with, a little misleading, since they were

preceded by a minimum of nine years of intense activity
beginning with his missionary work in Damascus right
after his conversion (Acts 9:20-22). Unfortunately, no
correspondence has survived from this period. The
Damascus activity, which lasted for over two years, was
no doubt continued elsewhere in the Arab kingdom of
Aretas IV, from whose attentions Paul escaped "in
a hamper" (he spent a good part of his life avoiding
death—"I die every day," I Corinthians 15:31). Luke
mentions a visit to Jerusalem in the company of Barnabas, a Cypriot who had dealt in property there, during
which he held extensive talks with Peter from whom, no
doubt, he learned much of Jesus and his last days in
the city—the passion story which he later "vividly
portrayed" to the Galatians (Galatians 3:1). During
this visit he received another vision of the risen Lord
who told him to leave the city and strengthened him
in his mission to the nations (Acts 22:17-21). This
visit ended with another attempt on his life and it was
deemed prudent to send him to his native city via the
port of Caesarea (Acts 9:26-30; Galatians 1:21).

For at least four years thereafter we hear nothing
of Paul, but we may be sure he was not inactive; in fact,
we hear almost by accident later on of Christian communities flourishing in just those regions to which Paul
tells us he went—namely in Syria, and Cilicia (Acts
15:23; Galatians 1:21). Tarsus was, and still is, an
easy enough journey from Antioch, and Paul must have
been in touch with developments in the latter center
where the "Church" was growing fast. There was evidently a shortage of trained leaders with the right
mental approach, for we find Barnabas sending to
Tarsus to invite Paul to come and work in the more
promising field of this the third largest city of the

Empire. Paul accepted and they worked there together for a year.

The Christian community in this great cosmopolitan center, with a population which could hardly have been much under half a million and an international reputation for vice, was a real microcosm of the Church then and in later times. "Greek" Christians had already taken the initiative in the mission field: the "deacons" of Acts 6 all have Greek names,[1] and one of them at least, Nicholas, was from Antioch, while the first to make a definite break *in practice* with Judaism were Cypriots and North Africans—which took place in this city and met with immediate success (Acts 11:20).[2] We should very much like to have been told more of these early Greek Christians, but Luke has been able to find space for the "Acts" of only one of them—Philip. Reading Luke's work, we have always to bear in mind how compressed it is—which requires some reading between the lines—and how the selection of material was dictated by very precise criteria which means that a great deal

[1] The word "deacon," *diakonos,* is in fact not used in this account, and from what follows it is evident that their activities were not confined to relieving the apostles of material and economic chores.

[2] Cyrene, an old Greek colony with a big Jewish population and a famous school of medicine, played an important part in the early years of the Church's history. There were Cyreneans present at the first Pentecost—they had a synagogue in Jerusalem (Acts 6:9)—and Mark mentions in his Gospel the two sons of the Simon who carried the cross for Jesus, Alexander and Rufus by name, known to the Roman community (Mark 15:21); the latter may in fact be the Rufus mentioned in Romans 16:13, whose mother was also a "mother" to Paul. Lucius the Cyrenean was one of the leaders of the Antioch Church (Acts 13:1). The role of the Cypriots will become evident from the narrative.

has been irretrievably lost. There must have been others like Philip who are, as one writer puts it, Agamemnons who never found a Homer, and we must be content with the little we have.

We recognize this community in the middle of a pagan and inhospitable city (which identified them by means of the derisive title "Christians," which has remained since) as the genuine missionary unit without regard for race, nation or social class and with an evident urge to expand and go out into the world. They realized that the Church is a body, an organism, a dynamic unity and that therefore it had continually to renew its cell structure in order to live. Thus we read that, in the course of a liturgical gathering, the church leaders —whose names are given in Acts 13:1—delegated Barnabas and Saul to go on a preaching mission to Cyprus and consolidate the work of the first evangelists who had fled there from the persecution connected with Stephen's death.

The Antioch Mission

It would be a mistake to think of these early missionaries as heady enthusiasts who plunged recklessly into activity without forethought. Take the mission to Cyprus. We have already seen how Cypriots had been among the first to break with the practice of speaking only to Jews (Acts 11:20), and it is noticeable that Barnabas and no doubt Mark, his cousin, had contacts in the island. We know that there were many Jews working in the copper mines which gave Cyprus its name, and Paul here was faithful to his usual plan of beginning with the synagogue in which, as a distinguished rabbi and pupil of Gamaliel, he had a right to speak. Here too the inestimable advantage of Roman citizenship gave him status in the eyes of the governor of this senatorial province, Sergius Paulus, who is known to us from an inscription found at Paphos and dating from the lifetime of Paul, and who became the first distinguished Roman convert that we know of (Cornelius was a mere centurion). It may be that he was one of those Godfearing pagans who in every city gathered round the synagogue, attracted by the moral purity of the Jewish faith, without, however, going so far as circumcision—what we might call associate or "third-order" Jews. At any rate, he had in his entourage a Jewish wizard called Bar-Jesus who was worsted in a direct encounter with Paul. This is the first of a series of glimpses which Luke gives us into the fascinating Jewish underworld of the first century—of quack doctors, magicians, wandering exorcists—familiar to us also from the papyri.

We do not know whether a visit to Asia Minor was part of the original plan. If not, it might have provided John Mark with some pretext for turning back, especially since in Cyprus he was more or less on home ground and the journey from the narrow malarial strip of coast up into the Taurus mountains, infested by robbers and wild animals, was quite a proposition. Events were in fact to prove his action prudent—Paul was in constant danger from the Jewish communities in the cities of the Anatolian upland and had the doubtful privilege of being taken for a god and stoned on the same day. Prudence of Mark's kind was never his strong point! We cannot help admiring the courage of a man who, after suffering the same fate which he had helped to inflict on Stephen and doubtless others, and then being thrown out of the city of Lystra, returned there and even came back a second time on another journey! Whenever we are tempted to think of Paul as a remote and ineffectual rabbi we should remember this—and many other indications of a moral and physical fibre of extraordinary toughness.

So the good news took root in Anatolia also, churches were set up, church leaders appointed and Paul kept in touch with them by correspondence—in this case the Letter to the Galatians.[3] The missionaries eventually got back to their base at Antioch after a much longer absence than Luke's compressed narrative might give us to understand—perhaps even as much as four years. We should note that it was in the course of this tour that Paul emerged as the leading missionary figure among the early Christians.

We, the Christians of today, owe a great debt to that first missionary community in Antioch, even though it has now disappeared completely from the scene. In the outskirts of the Turkish town of Antakya there is only a ruined Catholic chapel in a garden overgrown with weeds, now closed since there is no resident priest for the sixty or so families who worshiped there. Of the churches founded in the sweat and toil of those brave men—in Antioch in Pisidia, Iconium, Lystra, Derbe—nothing now remains, and the electronically amplified call to prayer of the muezzin from the tall white minaret of the mosque at Konya (Iconium), city of the dancing Dervishes, tells a different story. But we are living in a different age and each age, as one of the most famous of modern historians put it, is equidistant

---

[3] Other scholars held that this letter was addressed to Christian communities more to the north, in the district near Ankara (Ancyra) the modern capital of Turkey.

from God. Even though the circumstances have radically changed, the way of life and the task is the same.

Neither Jew nor Greek

By the end of his stay in Pisidian Antioch Paul must already have clearly envisaged a complete break with contemporary Judaism, as we can deduce from the peremptory "Behold, we turn to the Gentiles!" (Acts 13:46). The definitive rupture only came, however, with the visit to Corinth when Paul left the synagogue and took up lodgings next door in the house of Justus, a proselyte (Acts 18:6). Reading of how Konya was split into two camps through the divergent and mutually hostile missionary messages (14:4) might remind us of some sad chapters in modern missionary history and that the ecumenical movement first began in response to a need of this kind.

It will not be necessary to go into detail about how the Christian faith broke clear from its original wrappings in Judaism. As we have seen, Galatians gives us a fair idea of how bitterly the issue was fought out and how much it meant to Paul. The systematic attempts of the extreme Judaic element in the Jerusalem community to insist on circumcising new converts meant that the whole thing had to be thrashed out once and for all. In reading chapter 15 of Acts we should remember that there was probably nothing which could be described as a "council"—in the sense of an ecumenical council—and that in all probability Luke has combined here at least two meetings, just as in his Gospel (Luke 4:16-30) he seems to have combined two visits to Nazareth and presented them as if they were one. There are, in fact, two quite different issues:

the greater one of whether you could be a Christian without first being a circumcised Jew—a question of fundamental principle on which Paul would not move an inch—and the lesser one dealing with questions of legal purity arising from ritually "impure" Gentile Christians taking part in the community meals cheek by jowl with ritually "pure" Jewish Christians. Owing to the influence of James, the leader of the Jerusalem community, a working compromise was reached on this point, though in fact it was to play no important part in the Gentile communities established by Paul, as we can see by reading I Corinthians. Paul's emphasis in presenting the Christian life to converts was always on the complete freedom from the bonds of the past, both from a legal system, if they had been Jews, and from the bonds of sin and guilt. We should read Paul's own account of how strongly he reacted against Peter's lack of moral courage on the occasion of a visit to Antioch, probably after the Jerusalem meeting, when the leader of the apostolic Church began to shun the table fellowship of Gentile Christians at the urging of some Judaizing extremists who had arrived from Jerusalem—and even after the lesson implied in the conversion of the centurion Cornelius! (Galatians 2:11-14.) Paul had no patience with half-measures.

Into Europe

Paul and Barnabas returned to Antioch once this vital question of the freedom of a Christian man had been settled. At this point we meet for the first time with Silas, one of the two delegates of the Jerusalem community sent to promulgate the "apostolic decree" requesting Gentile Christians to avoid eating meat with the blood in it, meat of animals strangled or which had been offered to idols, and marriage within certain degrees of consanguinity common in the pagan world but especially abhorrent to Jews.[4] This Silas was a respected member of the Jerusalem Church, a Roman citizen like Paul and of Jewish origin (his name is in fact the Aramaic form of Saul!) who we are reasonably certain is the same as that Silvanus who was with Paul in Corinth (I Thessalonians 1:1; II Thessalonians 1:1; II Corinthians 1:19) and who, at a later stage, made a missionary journey of his own, taking with him the baptismal address which is part of our First Epistle of Peter (I Peter 5:12). After performing his task he stayed behind at Antioch, no doubt pressed by Paul, and accompanied him on his next pastoral tour.

The initial idea was merely a pastoral visitation of the communities founded during the previous journey. This, however, was shelved on account of a quarrel between Paul and Barnabas, his old colleague, which may have been due to the latter's abetting Peter's ambiguous behavior in Antioch. The result was an agreement to differ. Barnabas took Mark back to Cyprus while Paul and Silas took the land-route north through the Syrian Gates, the pass through the Amanus, round the Semitic Elbow and into his native Cilicia, then on to the churches founded three or four years before. At Lystra, scene of the stoning, he conscripted Timothy, son of a "mixed" marriage between a Greek father and

---

[4] The first two were ancient religious taboos based on the conviction that blood and breath are the two life-principles, and life belongs to God; see Genesis 9:4. Eating meat which had been offered to idols could be mistaken for participation in a sacrificial meal; see I Corinthians 10:18–20. These rules, however, soon proved impracticable, and Paul tacitly dropped them once his pagan mission was well under way.

a Jewish mother called Eunice. Paul showed his diplomatic ability, his willingness to compromise on the
unessential once the essential point had been won, in
having Timothy circumcised and in promulgating the
Jerusalem decree.

We should note at this point how Luke insists on
the role of the Spirit in these missionary enterprises.
Not just in the sense of an accession of new strength
in the face of opposition, suffering and danger, a sort
of supernatural endocrine gland providing new re-
sources when the unaided will seemed sapped and
spent, but in guiding them to a conclusion not originally
planned and foreseen. The blueprint of this missionary
progress had already been laid down in the very last
words spoken by Jesus to his followers before leaving
them—together with the promise of "power": "You
shall receive power when the Holy Spirit has come upon
you; and you shall be my witnesses in Jerusalem and in
all Judaea and Samaria and to the ends of the earth"
(Acts 1:8). Luke follows this order in his narrative
which begins in Jerusalem and ends in Rome. Here the
Paul-Silas mission is guided step by step, though we
are not told precisely how. They were somehow led
away from Bithynia and the Roman province of Asia
with its capital in Ephesus, toward the ancient shores of
Ilium sung by Homer which faced directly to Europe.
The last link was a dream or vision visitant, a man
recognized by his dress as Macedonian, inviting them
over from Troas, where they were staying, to the other
side. And so, perhaps in the spring of A.D. 50, some
twenty years after the crucifixion, the first organized
Christian mission came to Europe.

A short journey up from the port of Neapolis
brought the group to Philippi, a predominantly Roman

town built on the Via Egnatia, one of the great arterial ways of the Empire connecting Italy with the East. This city, named after the father of Alexander the Great, was given a new lease on life by the settlement of retired legionaries, beginning with some of those who encouraged the ambitions of Antony in the battle well known to readers of *Julius Caesar*. It was therefore a *colonia,* and Paul's readers would have understood perfectly his meaning when he wrote that "our home country is in heaven" (Philippians 3:20)—especially since he wrote in prison in the earthly "home country" of these distant colonials. It would certainly appear to have been a case of absence making the heart grow fonder, since Philippians is the warmest and the most tender letter Paul ever wrote.

It is noticeable that immediately after the invitation at Troas, Luke's narrative goes abruptly into the first person plural. This is the first of three excerpts from a travelogue which has been inserted into the narrative and if, as is highly probable, it was written by Luke himself, it would lend support to the theory that he either came from or was living in Philippi, since he joins up with Paul at Troas, accompanies him to this city but significantly is not put in prison with Paul and Silas. At a later stage (Acts 20:5) he falls in with Paul, again at Philippi, and stays with him up to the arrival in Jerusalem (21:17). The last extract begins in Caesarea on the eve of the ill-starred voyage to Rome of which he gives a vivid and circumstantial account (27:1–28:16). An origin in Philippi would also explain the rather dim view he took of the Athenians, since at this time, and for long before, there had been bitter rivalry between them and the Macedonians.[5]

There being no synagogue in Philippi, the small Jewish colony met outside the city by the River Ganga, no doubt choosing such a site for the same reason as had their forebears long before when they had sat down and wept "by the waters of Babylon" (Psalm 137), namely, for ritual washing which played an important part in their religious exercises. Among this group there was a wealthy woman, a proselyte, who came from Thyatira in Asia and dealt in the dyed cloth business, for which the latter city was famous—we know of well-organized dyers' guilds there as well as a flourishing Jewish colony. Lydia became an enthusiastic Christian, in fact the first European Christian we know by name, and gave hospitality to the missionaries. We do not know when and under what circumstances the Christian community was first established in the "home country" of Philippi, namely Rome, but it may be that the eucharist was first celebrated on European soil in Lydia's house, that it became therefore the first European "church."

We said previously that the faith, the "Way," was not a religion, was not a system. We now learn from a little incident that it is not (and ought not to become)

[5] Others prefer Antioch as his place of origin, chiefly on the basis of the short passage in the first person in the Western text of Acts 11:28, dealing with the arrival of Agabus the prophet. Cyrene has also been suggested on the (insufficient) grounds of a doubtful identification with the Loukios (Lucius) of Cyrene who was a church leader in Antioch (Acts 13:1), and the existence of an important school or university of medicine there—Luke being described in Colossians 4:14 as a doctor.

a vested interest, and that on the contrary it has constantly clashed with vested interests of different kinds. There was a young girl at Philippi who is described as being possessed by "a Python spirit"—meaning that she appeared to have a preternatural power similar to that of the miraculous python whose powers were taken over by Apollo at Delphi. Her ability to provide answers to questions put to her when in a trance, whether pathological or mere play-acting, had in any case been commercially exploited, and the cure or exorcism worked by Paul put her promoters at once out of business. The result was predictable: Paul and Silas were summarily flogged for being a public nuisance and thrown into prison, chained with their feet in the stocks, perhaps the fearful Roman *nervum*. In prison their apostolate continued until midnight when, as Luke tells us, a violent earthquake partially destroyed the building and they found themselves suddenly set free. The jailer wanted to kill himself, thinking his prisoners had escaped (he knew he would have been executed according to Roman practice), but Paul dissuaded him and took the occasion to instruct him in the essentials of the faith there and then in the torchlight and amid the smoking ruins. Here again is something typical of Paul. The jailer risked his life to take him and Silas to his house where their wounds were attended to and the whole family was baptized. Next day the police came to tell them they were free to go, but Paul would have none of this. They were both Roman citizens and had been beaten in defiance of the *Lex Porcia,* so back to the prison they went and insisted on the magistrates coming and apologizing. They did and, no doubt in a humbled tone, requested them to leave the city. The missionaries complied, but took their time about it.

After a journey of seventy miles along the Egnatian Way, they came to Salonika, then as now an important city (much of the old city has been destroyed by earthquake and fire). Here events followed more or less the same pattern: three weeks of relative peace—preaching in the synagogue and discussions with any willing to listen—and then the inevitable Jewish reaction, more violent this time since they enlisted the services of the marketplace rabble.[6] Paul stayed with a certain Jason, a name which was often taken by Dispersion Jews whose original name was Jesus, and in fact, if this is the same as the Jason mentioned in Romans 16:21, he would have been a relative of Paul's. A riot directed against "these men who have turned the world upside down" (17:6) was only averted by the direct intervention of the city authorities and Paul escaped another term in jail by his host raising bail, which, however, he must have forfeited, since Paul and his companion moved on by night to Beroea where the reception was much better.

We know from the letters written by Paul from Corinth to his Christians at Salonika that they had to put up with a real persecution even after he had left. This, combined with the fact that their instruction was abruptly terminated after a mere three weeks, caused them to have some wrong ideas on the imminence of the Lord's coming, and the main point of both letters is to help them to get this into clear perspective. Paul, after this time, insists more and more on the importance of terrestrial realities. Christianity is not a death-centered religion in the vague sense that we just hang

---

[6] The author uses a technical term here which would be very roughly equivalent to our "teddy-boys," "mods" or "rockers."

around in this world until we die, and hope for the best!
It is life-centered and this life is life *here and now,* but
directed, orientated decisively, to a life with God beyond death. The Christian life is this life as we know it
with a new dimension, the dimension of depth. And
this, for Paul, is not just a nice, up-in-the-air theory,
not after what he had gone through on this journey. He
was to sum it up very well in his letter to the Roman
community: "We rejoice in our sufferings, knowing that
suffering produces endurance, and endurance produces
character, and character produces hope, and hope does
not disappoint us, because God's love has been poured
out into our hearts through the Holy Spirit which has
been given to us" (Romans 5:3–5).

Christianity in the Marketplace

The troublemongers at Salonika pursued Paul to
nearby Beroea, and soon it was no longer safe for him
to stay anywhere in the North, so it was arranged that
he go on to Athens and there await developments with
the hope of being able to return some day to Macedonia
to complete the work he had begun. He fell in with this
plan though anxious to return to Salonika, and, probably after a sea voyage, found himself for the first time
in the city which was still in many ways the intellectual
center of the world, even if four centuries past its best.

Ostensibly things went on much as before—the
standard approach through the synagogue, finding his
best converts among the "God fearers," proselytes who
gathered round the local synagogue, thence making
contact whenever possible with the genuine pagan
environment. But his encounter in the marketplace, the
vast six acre area in the center of the city, with a group

of intellectuals, including no doubt pseudo-intellectuals and members of the "smart set," can be taken as marking a significant change, as the beginning of a new phase. If he had learned so far that the crucified Jesus was a stumbling block to Jews, he was now about to learn that for the Greeks he was folly. The encounter at Athens at a higher level, and at Corinth at a lower, with the Greeks, can be taken as a summing up of the whole encounter of the Christian faith with the world of then, or now, or any time. It might be worthwhile considering briefly some aspects of that encounter.

Ignorance of history, as Sainte-Beuve remarked, always makes us calumniate our own age. It is probable that the world of the first century, as it emerges in the scores of papyri letters dealing with the ordinary affairs of life, in the writings of moralists and public figures, artists and poets and, here and there, in the letters of Paul, was, if anything, worse than that of the twentieth. It would be easy to draw up lists of quotations illustrating vice of every kind, the perversion of family life, the general loss of confidence in the possibility of a genuine spiritual life—to point to the mosaics in the Baths of Caracalla in Rome or the House of the Mysteries in submerged Pompeii and then go on to read the first chapter of Romans. What is more significant is that the moral sense—and we are speaking of public morality— was probably more thoroughly anaesthetized then: we do not, as a rule, expose unwanted children or permit open defense of certain forms of socially destructive sexual behavior, and, of course, there was slavery. We can, therefore, understand the admiration of Tacitus for the unspoilt moral sense of the Teutons in his *Germania* in contrast to the decaying morality of imperial Rome.

At a deeper level, however, there was a kind of

emptiness, a lack of dimension in that twilight, post-rational world. The official religion, emperor worship, in the person of a notorious pervert like Tiberius or a criminal lunatic like Caracalla, was for most people just a sick joke. The old gods and goddesses were dead but their ghosts haunted men's minds. Religion was, in the main, an instrument of fear and not of joy; the kind of fear that Lucretius, in his *De Rerum Natura,* written about a century earlier, tried to exorcise with his atomistic materialism and the reduction of everything to blind chance. If it is true that the task of religion has always been to provide an alternative to death, it would appear that most people seemed to find that alternative unacceptable; the only thing was to make hay while the sun shone before the *nox perpetua una dormienda.*[7] A contemporary of Lucretius and Catullus, known and quoted by Paul, puts into the mouth of his impious man a very fair representation of this point of view, expressed by means of the predominantly atomistic philosophical jargon of the day:

By chance we came into being
And after this we will be as if we had not existed,
For the breath in our nostrils is smoke
And our thinking a spark at the beating of the heart;
When this is extinguished the body goes to ashes
And the spirit is dispersed into air . . .
And our life will pass away like traces of a cloud.
. . . .
Come, then, let us enjoy the real good things,
Let us use created things as in youth, with ardor,

[7] From one of Catullus' poems: "The sun can continually go down and return, but once our brief light has gone there remains but one perpetual night for sleeping."

Regale ourselves with costly wine and perfume!
Let the flower of our springtime not pass away from us!
Let us crown ourselves with rose petals before they fade!
Let no one be missing at our orgy,
Leaving on every side signs of our joy —
This is our portion, this is our lot!   (Wisdom 2:2–9)

This is one side of the picture. On the other side there would be the extraordinary development of the so-called mystery religions, like that of Eleusis a few miles from Athens, which claimed to place union with God within the reach of the *mystes,* the initiate, and which helped to break down class distinctions by admitting all, even slaves, on an equal footing; there were the private mysticisms of Orphic and Pythagorean inspiration like that of the wandering sage Apollonius who, it appears, visited Athens about the same time as Paul; all these and other phenomena witnessed to a great thirst for salvation in the world of the first century. More significant because more influential, there was Stoicism, *the* philosophical and religious idiom of the day, which had begun three and a half centuries earlier in the very marketplace where Paul was proclaiming the Word. Paul was a contemporary of the famous Stoic philosopher Seneca whose brother Gallio was proconsul of the Roman province of which Corinth was capital at the time of Paul's visit there. The discourse on Mars' Hill (Acts 17:22–31) is interesting since it appears to be an attempt to see how far the Christian message could be made to agree with the tenets of Stoicism, the ascendant philosophy of the day—themes such as the unity of mankind, the pointlessness of idols, the divine atmosphere in which man lived his life (for Stoics the world was a divine, living organism of which man was, so to speak, a cell), the noble demands of human reason—but the idea of a dead body coming to life again, in the face of the "standard" Greek asceticism of getting away from the body (*to soma sema*—"the body is a tomb"), was too much for them to swallow, and the whole case collapsed. Yet the attempt continued and continues to the present day—suffice it to think of Origen and Platonism, St. Augustine and Neo-Platonism, St. Thomas Aquinas and Aristotle, Christians of different persuasions like Marcel and Bultmann, and existentialism.

At Corinth, to which he moved in a decidedly disillusioned state of mind as we know from his first letter, it was still the Greek pagan world but on a different level; for, as Paul told them with his accustomed candor: "Not many of you were wise according to worldly standards, not many were powerful, not many were of noble birth" (I Corinthians 1:26). His difficulties were by no means over: while among the intellectuals and pseudo-intellectuals of Athens he had been dubbed a peddler in second-hand ideas (Acts 17:18), in this city of athletes (the Isthmian Games were held there) and volatile conversationalists, "his bodily presence is puny and his speech of no account" (II Corinthians 10:10). At any rate, he made no attempt to repeat the Athens experiment but set out from the start to speak of "the foolishness of the cross" and to go straight to the all-important question of living the life "in Christ," not just talking about it. Of this we shall see something later.

Luke tells us in Acts of the friendship which he struck up with a Jewish couple, Aquila and Priscilla, who were in the same trade as he—they were to become excellent Christians and do great work—of a further stage in the break with the synagogue, the usual riot, and of his being comforted in a dream or vision, a kind of extension of the presence of the risen Lord who had first appeared to him some fifteen years before. The rest we have to glean from the correspondence written in the main from Ephesus and the surrounding district; he sent them at least four letters of which only two have survived. After a stay of about two years, having long since given up hope of returning to work in Salonika, he made his way back to base in Antioch.

The Ephesus Mission

When the weather was again fit for travelling, Paul set off on the land route northward to keep his promise of coming back to Ephesus. While he was on his way, a sensation had been caused in the community of the latter city by the arrival from Alexandria, the great center of learning, of a brilliant Christian named Apollos, whom Luke seems to have known well and admired. This man evidently played an important part in the history of the early Church but one which is, in many respects, still rather mysterious. He was at the head of a group, organized in twelve like the apostles, which followed the teaching of the Baptist, evidently differing to a considerable extent from Christianity since he had to be instructed and baptized into the full Christian faith—by Paul's friends, Aquila and his wife. He missed Paul at Ephesus, having moved across to Corinth where he figures in the second stage of Christian instruction and initiation in that city, though, to judge by some remarks in Paul's first letter, he, Paul, was not entirely happy about either the nature or the opportuneness of the kind of instruction he was giving. It has been suggested that Apollos may have been a disciple of the great Alexandrian scholar Philo, the learned Jew; that his party may have had connections with the Jewish religious order of Qumran and that he may have written the Letter to the Hebrews. All of this, however, is uncertain.

Viewing the ruins of Efes (Ephesus) today, a fifty-mile dolmus-taxi ride south of Izmir (Smyrna), it is difficult to imagine the splendor and squalor of the great city of Paul's day. Little remains of the *Artemision,* temple to the goddess Artemis, greatest of the seven wonders of the ancient world which, according to the story, had been built after its predecessor was burned down by a madman on the night Alexander the Great was born (356 B.C.). The great harbor, now silted up, and the overland routes brought traders from as far away as China and Spain; and there was a constant flow of pilgrims who came to worship at the shrine of the Great Mother.

Paul made Ephesus his center for the next three years, though of course he did not content himself with remaining in the city all this time. It was during this period that the seven churches of the Apocalypse were founded (Revelation 2–3), and several journeys and missions were organized in the direction of Europe. We see Paul perfecting his missionary method: very soon came the predictable break with the synagogue, after which he rented a lecture hall during the off hours (between 11 a.m. and 4 p.m. when it was considered too hot to work) and taught in this way for about two years. We see him organizing at the same time various well trained missionary teams—we know, for example, that a group under Epaphras evangelized Colossae (how well we may judge by the high standard implied in the letter to that church), Timothy and Erastus were sent into Macedonia, there were Gaius and Aristarchus, Titus who was to become bishop in Crete and many others. All this region of the Meander basin was to become the key center of Christianity in the East for many a century.

As readers of Shakespeare's *The Comedy of Errors* will remember, Ephesus was the center of the magical arts in the ancient world and it was not surprising that Paul should have had a round with a group of Jewish exorcists, an incident which Luke relates with a good deal of quiet, ironical humor (Acts 19:11–19). The main point in these exorcisms was to hit on the name of the demon supposed to be in the one possessed, since knowledge of the name signified power over the demon. Quite a number of magical papyri have survived including the great Paris Magical Papyrus, which is 133 feet long and dates back to the end of the third century! In this case the magic turned against them and the conclusion was comical rather than tragic, but it is significant that Paul speaks more than once of the oppressive fear of supernatural evil spirits, "the powers of darkness," in his letter to Ephesus (e.g. 6:12). The whole episode ended with a spectacular burning of the books.[8]

---

[8] This was, and remained right down to the end of the Middle Ages, the established form for renouncing magical practices, as we can see from Marlowe's *Doctor Faustus,* though the latter's decision to do so came a little too late. The connection between Judaism and the occult arts remained strong down to modern times, at least in the popular imagination—Mephistopheles has a Hebrew name, and magic formulae were usually in that language or one closely related, even down to the last popular survivals such as our *abracadabra,* which means "word of power."

Most of Luke's space is given over to an account, very vivid and circumstantial, of the riot in the amphitheater instigated by a certain Demetrius, spokesman for the manufacturers of objects of piety connected with the temple and its goddess—another case of Christianity clashing with vested interests. The occasion was probably the great spring pilgrim festival when the city would be full of tens of thousands come from all over Asia Minor and beyond to honor the Great Mother, goddess of the fertile earth. Seeing their chance of profit in danger, they got together a rabble in the theater, most of whom, as our historian drily tells us, didn't even know why they were there. Only a bit of quick thinking and *sangfroid* on the part of the town clerk avoided a major disaster. At any rate Paul was safe for the moment, but it was evidently impossible for him to continue for the time being in Ephesus, so he left for Macedonia and Southern Greece, then doubled back to avoid being ambushed. Luke again joined up with the band at Philippi, and they crossed back over to Troas, from which Paul had first set out for Europe eight years before.

Luke now gives us an eyewitness account of an eucharistic service held at Troas which none present would have been likely to forget. It was an evening Mass, the Saturday evening which opened the Christian "sabbath," namely Sunday—the Jewish liturgical day began in the evening. There would have been reading from the scriptures and prayers, followed by the sermon or homily. The meeting was, then as always in the early days, in a private house, and people sat around in quite an informal way, rather different from our rows of benches all in line. One youngster was even sitting on a window sill at a good height, a rather imprudent position as it turned out. The sermon was rather long that warm spring evening, and Eutychus (his name means "Lucky"), who had dozed off, fell and was killed, a lesson to all who sleep during sermons. Paul, perhaps feeling himself to some extent responsible, bent over him and restored him to life. The eucharistic service proper followed, and afterwards Paul went on talking informally into the small hours.

After a week in Troas the sea journey continued by small stages. Ephesus had to be missed, but Paul summoned the church leaders, no doubt including his friends Aquila and Priscilla, to Miletus where he addressed them as he thought for the last time. He was under no illusions as to the distinct possibility of violent death when he reached Jerusalem, and this gives an urgency and moving power to his discourse which should be read in its entirety (Acts 20:17–38). The journey continued; at Patara they picked up a cargo vessel bound for Tyre where again they spent seven days, met on the beach for prayers and mutual encouragement, and so on to Caesarea. Here the party were the guests of Philip (the evangelist of Acts, not the apostle), evidently a good friend of Luke. Here Paul received the last of many prophetic warnings of the sufferings awaiting him in Jerusalem—this time from Agabus, whom Luke had already met at Antioch on an earlier occasion. But Paul was determined to be there for the feast of Pentecost; perhaps he wanted to hand in the collection for the mother church on the twenty-fifth anniversary of the first Christian Pentecost. They set off on the last stage of their journey and, upon arrival in the city, stayed with Mnason, a member of the Christian Cypriot colony there.

Part V
The Man
in His
Correspondence

WHY did we have to retell this story? Not just for the sake of the story but in order to prove a point, the point made in the previous section. If Paul had been just a theoretician, that is, a theologian (which he was not, despite the immense number of learned volumes written about him) we might have been tempted to say after reading that section, as in fact so many do: "Religion's all right in theory, but it's no good for living; it just doesn't square up to the demands of our three-dimensioned existence, of our *real life.*"

Real life! What his story tells us on every page is that if our "religion" is not in and of our real life, we had better get rid of it as quickly as possible. It proves the truth of his apparently exaggerated claim: "For me to be alive means Christ," for the possibility of a Christianity separate from real life never occurred to Paul. It is obvious that we learn far better what Christianity (union with God through Christ living in the Church) means from knowing and living with a person for whom these things are real (in fact the basic reality) than just reading about them in a book or thinking about them. Sufficient to remember what the contemporaries of men like Philip Neri or Francis de Sales said about them, or the impact of a truly Christ-centered life on those who suffered with them in the Nazi prisons of people like Monsignor Kolbe or Pastor Bonhoeffer. When we think of it, the pattern was the

74

same in the life of Christ himself. It was in what he did and, above all, in what he *was,* rather than in what he said, that those who lived with him gradually and almost without reflection began to be aware of the overwhelming presence of God. This is the theme of Mark's Gospel in particular—the Mark who let Paul down as we saw but who stood by him in prison later on—in which question after question is put about the mysterious identity of the central figure, until we come to the *dénouement,* the answer, in Peter's confession of faith and the transfiguration, "the glory of God in the face of Christ." For Paul, who saw the transfigured Christ on the mountain as the counterpart of Moses transfigured after his encounter with God on Sinai, the object of our existence is to share in that transfiguration, to come into God's presence, to see him as Moses did face to face; but this has to come about through a gradual transformation in our here-and-now existence, not just as a vague object of hope: "For we all, with unveiled face, beholding the glory of the Lord, are being changed into his likeness from one degree of glory to another; for this comes from the Lord who is the Spirit" (II Corinthians 3:18).

It is significant that this comes in the same letter in which, writing from Ephesus and to a Church which had snubbed and insulted him, he says: "We should like you to know, brothers, what we had to put up with in Asia; for we were so utterly, unbearably crushed that we despaired of life itself—we felt we had received the sentence of death" (II Corinthians 1:8-9).

This leads on to his correspondence, for it is here that we see this transforming force at work upon the raw material of his own existence and of those for whom he felt himself responsible. Before we go on to see how this worked out in practice, however, we had better clear up some misunderstandings and make one or two preliminary observations about the letters as a whole.

They were not, needless to say, written at a desk in the more or less leisurely way we write our letters. We have to remember that in general for the ancients the ear was more important than the eye. Thus people did not, as a rule, read to themselves. We remember that Philip *heard* the Ethiopian reading Isaiah in his chariot (Acts 8:30), and there is the incident in St. Augustine's *Confessions* in which he came upon Ambrose reading silently and was evidently taken aback. Paul's letters were composed and dictated aloud and read aloud to communities in which there would certainly be a good number who could not read.

This point of dictation is important. Paul usually only signed the letters with his own hand. Thus, at the end of the second letter to Salonika, he adds: "I, Paul, add this greeting with my own hand. This is the mark in every letter of mine; it is the way I write" (II Thessalonians 3:17). Similarly in the Galatians letter he adds: "See with what large letters I am writing to you with my own hand." We find similar remarks at the end of several other letters, obviously with the idea of reassuring them that the letter was really from him. Dictation was a long business since it is not likely that any of his temporary secretaries knew shorthand;[1] from what we know of his amazingly full life we can imagine him either walking up and down, mostly late at night,

---

[1] Tiro had worked out an efficient system of *notae*, or shorthand, for recording his friend Cicero's speeches which passed into general use, chiefly for legal proceedings.

measuring out the phrases to suit the speed of his secretary, perhaps with some impatience and the occasional gesticulation, or dictating while his hands were busy at the loom—the hands he held up to show the leaders of the Ephesus community that he had always worked for his living (Acts 20:34). The fact that no secretary would normally be able to do more than an hour or two at a stretch would imply that there might be some break in continuity in the composition of the letters—which in fact is confirmed by quite a number of rather violent transitions and a few *non sequiturs* here and there. And, of course, there would be people calling in to see him and breaking the association of ideas so important in this slow, deliberate oral form of composition.

Many of the difficulties involved in understanding Paul's thought, alluded to by Peter as we saw at the beginning, are due to compression. This was due not just to psychological reasons—Paul's explosive nature which eschewed calm, rational discourse—but also to the oral technique to which he was constrained, to the shortage of time and also, we should not omit to mention, the price of papyrus.[2] Thus, while his letters vary in length—from the note to Philemon, which was

---

[2] Papyrus, from which we get our word "paper," was made by gluing together fibrous strips of the plant of that name which grew abundantly in the Nile valley. Only one side was prepared for writing on by smoothing with a shell or a piece of ivory. There were, as Pliny tells us in his *Natural History*, five varieties each with its own price, of which the most popular in Paul's day seems to have been called "amphitheater paper." Coarser varieties were sold by weight not by sheet. Writing was usually with a sharpened goose quill and ink was made from glue and lampblack. Some ink, in a solidified state, was found in the inkwells at Qumran dating from at least a century before Paul.

more a postcard than a letter and would have taken up just one small sheet of papyrus, to the first letter to Corinth and the one to Rome, which are nearly twenty times longer—even the longer ones are crowded with ideas and waste no time on trivialities. This means we have to be constantly alert in reading them if we wish to follow what he is saying.

They are real letters to real people, many of whom were personally known to Paul, and they therefore reveal a real personality, since this is only possible in communication with people known and loved. Though only four of the thirteen are addressed to individuals, the rest always end with a list of friends whom he wishes to salute personally; Paul had a genius for friendship.[3] The fact remains, however, that, as a whole, the correspondence is addressed to Christian communities and cannot therefore be compared with strictly personal letters, such as those which Cicero wrote to his friend Tiro. We do not know to what extent Paul inherited this idea of exchanging letters and of passing them round (as we see was the case from Colossians 4:16); but it certainly became a normal feature in the life of the early communities, as we know from surviving examples, such as Clement of Rome's letter to Corinth, Bishop Ignatius of Antioch's extant correspondence to neighboring communities, that of the persecuted Christians of Vienne and Lyons in France written in 177 to the Churches of Asia and Phrygia, and the like.

What is important for us to notice is that Paul has

---

[3] In the concluding chapter of Romans (which some take to be a separate letter of recommendation for the deaconess Phoebe) he greets twenty-eight friends: twenty-one men and seven women.

before his eyes as he writes a certain well-known community gathered together in the house of a leading member for worship, in the course of which liturgical function his letter would be read. He therefore speaks as if present and presiding and often has a special word for different classes of people—church leaders, deacons, women, children. This explains, too, why so often we find liturgical elements in the letters. They almost always open with a prayer for the church assembled— "I give thanks to God always for you"—and contain very many snatches and doxologies familiar to us from the liturgy such as "Through Christ our Lord." The conclusion of many letters also looks very much like the conclusion of a service; thus we know that the cry "Our Lord, come!" (*marana tha!*) was a regular part of early church services, and of the eucharist in particular,[4] and Paul ends his first letter to Corinth with the words:

> Our Lord, come!
> The grace of the Lord Jesus be with you!
> My love be with you all in Christ Jesus. Amen.

There are also hymns such as the one about Christ in the first letter to Timothy (3:16); and the frequency with which Paul speaks of the Holy Spirit surely has something to do with the fact that it was when they were gathered together in worship, and in particular for the eucharist, that the early Christians experienced this supernatural presence. We know from I Corinthians in

---

[4] We find it here in the early Church book called *The Teaching of the Twelve Apostles,* which is first century. This expectation would correspond to the Jewish Passover in which the desire for the Messiah's coming finds strong expression.

particular that the spiritual or charismatic gifts which formed such a prominent part of church life then were exercised during the liturgical gatherings.

What scholars call the "Pauline Canon" consists of the collection of his extant correspondence as forming an important part of the New Testament. Not all, of course, have survived and it is not impossible, absolutely speaking, that one or other might turn up some day, in the unexpected kind of way that the Qumran scrolls or the Khenoboskion "Sayings of Jesus" came to light.[5] At the same time, it is unlikely that anything very important has been lost: the definitive collection was put together and venerated very early, as we know from Peter's second letter (3:15) and that of Clement of Rome to Corinth (about A.D. 90); and the other letters which we know from internal evidence he wrote to the Corinthian Christians may have been built into the present letters, while the letter to Laodicea, mentioned in Colossians 4:16, is probably our Ephesians. When we think that only little more than half of Cicero's correspondence has survived, and he was a better known man than Paul, we have every reason to be thankful.

Doubts have been raised off and on for centuries as to whether Paul actually wrote all the letters which have a place in the Church's New Testament canon. The Epistle to the Hebrews presents a special problem

[5] The Qumran scrolls were discovered in 1947 and subsequent years. The "Sayings of Jesus" referred to were discovered by accident at Nag Hammadi (ancient name, Khenoboskion) in Egypt probably in 1945, and are sometimes referred to as the "Gospel of Thomas." The collection was probably put together by a somewhat heretical Christian group, but some few of the sayings could well go back to Jesus.

since it was doubted from the earliest times whether Paul wrote it, and in language and ideas it stands in a class of its own. It was probably written by someone either trained by Paul or close to him; we might think of a missionary like Apollos or Barnabas or Silas. The two letters to Timothy and the one to Titus (usually called the Pastoral Epistles) are also in a class of their own, since they come from the last phase of Paul's life —his second imprisonment under Nero—and were written under circumstances of extreme hardship, in which he quite likely had to leave the actual writing entirely to a friend; they also have a purpose which is different from the others and are the only ones (apart from the letter to Philemon) addressed to individuals. Doubts are also expressed as regards the second letter to Thessalonians, Ephesians and Colossians, but the reasons adduced are not sufficient for us to set aside the evidence from early Church writers, which inspired their acceptance as genuine in the first place. Linguistic analysis and statistics, aided by a Mercury computer, have recently renewed speculation and discussion on this subject and brought it to the attention of the public through a sensational Sunday newspaper article, "A Computer Challenges the Church," though the intemperate language used generated more heat than light, and tended rather to obscure the value of this kind of analysis as a useful adjunct to the scientific work which scholars had been carrying on quietly during the preceding century. In this question we have to take account not only of tradition and the usual internal arguments, but also the amount of freedom given to a secretary, which could be considerable if the circumstances warranted it, the purpose of the letter, different methods of composition and the use of traditional and liturgical matter—this latter especially in letters intended to be read at a liturgical gathering.

The story as we have traced it down to the autumn of A.D. 58, when he arrived in Jerusalem to face a future full of uncertainty, can be followed indirectly in the first batch of his letters written during these years— those to the communities in Salonika, the Galatian towns, Corinth and Rome.[6] It is here that we can study the sources, the mainspring of the history, and get the best idea of his personality. We may not find much in the way of interesting personal detail, such as we do in the seven hundred and ninety-six extant letters of Cicero, except for details such as the request to Philemon to get a room ready for him, or to Timothy to bring the cloak and writing materials he had left at Troas. They confirm the impression we get from Luke's story—a man of contrasts and even extremes, a combination of strength and tenderness. Of the physical basis we know little and learn nothing significant here. The distance he traveled, the continual physical and mental strain and the physical violence he withstood hardly make us think of a weak-kneed intellectual! We have to read imaginatively between the lines when Luke includes in his history a long account of the two hour riot in Ephesus, but passes over in a sentence the two years spent teaching each day between 11 a.m. and 4 p.m. when everyone else was resting, or when later he tells us apropos of Paul's imprisonment in Caesarea ". . . but when *two years* had elapsed, Felix was succeeded by Portius Festus . . ." Paul is driven by his

[6] See Table on pp. 117-18 for the chronology of the letters.

detractors to give us something resembling an auto-
biography in the second letter to Corinth:

> ... with far greater labors, far more imprison-
> ments, with countless beatings, and often near
> death. Five times I have received at the hands of
> the Jews the forty lashes less one. Three times I
> have been beaten with rods; once I was stoned.
> Three times I have been shipwrecked; a night and
> a day I have been adrift at sea; on frequent jour-
> neys, in danger from rivers, danger from robbers,
> danger from my own people, danger from Gen-
> tiles, danger in the city, danger in the wilderness,
> danger at sea, danger from false brethren; in toil
> and hardship, through many a sleepless night, in
> hunger and thirst, often without food, in cold and
> exposure ... (II Corinthians 11:23–27)

In addition to this, we have to remember that for a
part of this time he was a very sick man. He tells the
Galatians that a bad illness had been the occasion of
his coming to them in the first place (4:13) and it is
not difficult to deduce from the Corinth letters that he
arrived in that city sick and mortally tired (e.g., I
Corinthians 2:3). We have no means of knowing
whether the "thorn in the flesh" to which he refers
(II Corinthians 12:5) was, as some have supposed, a
recurrent ailment of a particularly painful and embar-
rassing kind—something like epilepsy, malaria, dysen-
tery or astigmatism; it might seem more natural, in
view of his referring to it as "a messenger of Satan," to
think of a moral temptation which assailed him continually. We know at any rate that, despite the tremendous hardships which beset him, he chastised his
body and subdued it (I Corinthians 9:26) in order, as

he says, to complete what was lacking in the sufferings of Christ.

In the first of his letters, those to the Thessalonians —in which, incidentally, Silas and Timothy cooperated, as the titles tell us—there is the sensation, as we read them, of a new world full of inner conviction and coherence which has come into existence. Here at last, one feels, there is something which can withstand the force and pressures of evil in the world. Right from the opening greeting: "Grace and peace!" we have the feeling of a real unity not based on self-interest as is the case with other societies but on real love, charity, something almost inconceivable in the world at that time or, for that matter, at any other. This is what a second century Christian letter will call "the new blood and spirit." In comparison with this the problem of the time and circumstances of the Second Coming, with which the letters are largely concerned but which is hardly a problem for us, is seen to be quite secondary.

The letter to the Galatians is the most personal of all and the one in which we detect most clearly Paul's character and ideals. The central idea has been discussed in an earlier section,[7] and as an introduction to it we find an important autobiographical passage dealing with the period from just before his conversion, down to the Antioch incident. More important for us is the *meaning* of events, how Paul interpreted them at the deeper level of the mind and the heart. One phrase is particularly significant: "I through the Law died to the Law that I might live to God" (2:19).

As we have already suggested, this is valid not just for Paul but for the life of any Christian: the passage

[7] See pp. 34–36.

from the negative of a legal observance—just observing a system of rules and regulations—to the positive of *living to God*. This for Paul is a being set free—not in the sense that the Christian can do what he likes (this was a common misunderstanding in the permissive atmosphere of Corinth, "all things are lawful for me") but by enabling him to exercise his freedom on an altogether higher plane of action. "For freedom *Christ* has set me free" he says—you can't do this yourself; it is only possible through union with Christ in death and resurrection: "I have been crucified with Christ; it is no longer I who live but Christ lives in me; and the life I now live in the flesh I live by faith in the Son of God who loved me and gave himself for me" (2:20). The old life ends on the cross; the new one begins with the resurrection.

For Paul, it is only through this identifying ourselves with Christ that we get the strength to go beyond self, the self-centered existence which is common to all nature below man and also to unredeemed man as part of that world—an animal cannot help being selfish (which may possibly explain why we use the phrase "the rat-race!"). We do not rise above this level by following a system but by identifying ourselves with Christ on the cross—Paul and the apostles, the untold number of martyrs of the persecutions which were just beginning at the end of Paul's life, did not die for a *system!*

Why (Paul will ask the Corinthians a little later) am I in peril every hour? I protest, brethren, by my pride in you which I have in Christ Jesus our Lord, I die every day! What do I gain if, humanly speaking, I fought with beasts at Ephesus? If the dead

are not raised "Let us eat and drink, for tomorrow
we die!"   (I Corinthians 15:30–32)

Already, at the time of writing to the Galatians, he can
speak of bearing on his body the marks of Jesus, that is,
of the flogging which had been his lot during the visit to
Lystra.

The first of the letters to the Corinthians reflects his
state of mind after the Athens failure, which was not to
be by any means the end of his troubles. He had to put
up with quite some abuse, to the effect that he was
undersized and insignificant, a poor speaker and a
braggart (II Corinthians 10:10 etc.). Even his decision
to leave any attempt at expressing the Christian message
in the framework of a philosophy, a natural reaction
after Athens, was interpreted as putting him on a
lower level than other teachers whom Paul refers to sar-
castically as "super-apostles" (II Corinthians 11:5).
Put bluntly, many of them felt that his presence was
superfluous. Hence his moving approach:

Already you are filled! Already you have become
rich! Without us you have become kings! And
would that you did reign so that we might share
the rule with you! For I think that God has ex-
hibited us apostles as last of all, like men sentenced
to death; because we have become a spectacle to
the world, to both angels and men. We are fools
for Christ's sake, but you are wise in Christ. We
are weak but you are strong. You are held in
honor but we in disrepute. To the present hour we
hunger and thirst, we are ill-clad and buffeted and
homeless, and we labor, working with our hands.
When reviled, we bless; when persecuted, we en-
dure; when slandered, we try to conciliate; we
have become, and are now, as the refuse of the

world, the offscouring of all things. I do not write this to make you ashamed, but to admonish you as my beloved children. For though you have countless guides in Christ, you do not have many fathers.   (I Corinthians 4:8–15)

Both these letters give us a good idea of what Paul meant by "my anxiety for all the churches"; the first one in particular is to a great extent dedicated to solving personal and communal problems: factions which had cropped up in the community (1:10–17) connected with partisan zeal for particular evangelizers (3:1–15), a case of gross immorality (5:1–8), some Christians refusing to have their differences settled out of court (6:1–8), courtship and married life (7), food offered to idols (8), disorders in the weekly eucharistic meeting (11) and the like. This shows us in practice the meaning of that other-directed and therefore God-directed love which Paul praises in ecstatic language in chapter 13. It is by this kind of commitment to "real life" that the transformation, the transfiguration, takes place:

The word of the cross is folly to those who are perishing, but to us *who are being saved* it is the power of God.

We are the aroma of Christ to God among those *who are being saved* and among those who are perishing, to one a fragrance from death to death, to the other a fragrance *from life to life*.

We all, with unveiled face, beholding the glory of the Lord, *are being changed* into his likeness from one degree of glory to another.

But as we have seen more than once, Paul is a realist,

not just a facile coiner of the fine phrase—the test of
fire is always experience:

> We have this treasure in earthen vessels, to show
> that the transcendent power belongs to God and
> not to us. We are afflicted in every way, but not
> crushed; perplexed, but not driven to despair;
> persecuted but not forsaken; struck down, but not
> destroyed; always carrying in the body the death of
> Jesus so that the life of Jesus may also be mani-
> fested in our bodies. For while we live we are
> always being given up to death for Jesus' sake, so
> that the life of Jesus may be manifested in our
> mortal flesh.   (II Corinthians 4:7–11)

This is part of the Christian paradox: weakness—
strength, death—life, for it is nothing else than the
paradox of Christ who "was crucified in weakness, but
lives by the power of God" (II Corinthians 13:4).

Romans, finally, is much less personal since addressed to a community which Paul did not found and
was not acquainted with. Though certainly a real letter,
it is, like Ephesians, rather more like a treatise in which
he works out calmly the line of thought he had composed in some haste and agitation in the letter to the
Galatians. Written at Corinth during the winter of 57,
it lays down the groundplan of the Christian life: what
he conceives the good news to be, the world to which
it is addressed and which needs it desperately, how it is
appropriated by faith like that of Abraham, baptism as
the passage into a new dimension of existence. All of
this is, of course, personal insofar as it sprang directly
from his own experience and is meant to be lived out in
practice; so, for example, his views on the destiny of the
Jews in God's plan within history open with a highly
personal statement of how deep his attachment to his

own race remained despite what he had gone through (9:1–5). It is also possible that the passage in which he speaks of the hopelessness of trying to keep up continually with the demands of conscience, of "being good" without the grace of God, and which ends with the *cri de cœur:* "Wretched man that I am! Who will deliver me from this body of death?" reflects indirectly the moral struggles of his early life before his conversion, particularly during adolescence (7:7–25).[8] At any rate, the last word is one of optimism:

> If God is for us, who is against us? He who did not spare his own Son but gave him up for us all, will he not also give us all things with him? Who shall bring any charge against God's elect? It is God who justifies; who is to condemn? It is Jesus Christ who died, yes, who was raised from the dead, who is at the right hand of God, who intercedes for us. Who shall separate us from the love of Christ? Shall tribulation, or distress, or persecution, or famine, or nakedness, or peril, or the sword? As it is written, "For thy sake we are being killed all the day long; we are regarded as sheep to be slaughtered." No, in all these things we are more than conquerors through him who has loved us. For I am sure that neither death, nor life, nor angels, nor principalities, nor things present, nor things to come, nor powers, nor height, nor depth, nor anything else in all creation, will be able to separate us from the love of God in Christ Jesus our Lord.   (8:31–39)

---

[8] *Indirectly* because it is more in keeping with Paul's usual methods and the context here to take the *ego* as primarily impersonal, that is, referring to man as such, man under a preceptive religion. But also, knowing Paul's intensely personal approach to religion, it would appear too relentless a scruple to exclude any autobiographical undertone.

Part VI
Then and Now

IF we could imitate the Seven Sleepers of Ephesus and make a miraculous journey through time, back to the Church of that city during Paul's three year stay there, we might find the experience not only strange but rather trying. We might even wonder whether it was the same religion or something quite different. There would be no Benediction, no Exposition of the Blessed Sacrament, no rosary, no religious orders, not even any nuns. We would look in vain for a confession "box" in the local house-church and might have some difficulty in recognizing the eucharistic service (in the absence of vestments, warning bell and the rest) as the familiar Mass.

Notwithstanding all of this, it would be the same Christian life, the same Church; only in order to see this, we should be obliged to dig beneath the surface and sort out what is essential to that life and what is only marginal. Our usual criterion for determining the status of a Catholic Christian (for example, when the question of marriage crops up) is the existence of a baptismal certificate, while the usual criterion for what is usually called a "good Catholic" is presence in a particular building during an act of worship once a week, that is, on Sundays. Correctly understood, these criteria are excellent since they take us at once to the heart of our faith in the great Church sacraments of baptism and the eucharist, and if anything is essential in the Christian message, these are. Leaving, therefore, on one side any attempt at a systematic presentation of Paul's doctrine on the sacraments, the Church and other aspects of life in Christ— which will be dealt with in other volumes of this series —we might attempt an unsystematic and informal link-up between what being a Christian meant *then* and what it ought to mean *now,* which will involve trying to pinpoint what is essential to that life as opposed to what is marginal.

The Christian in Church

Christians have always been identified by their attendance at a weekly liturgical meeting. The earliest accusations leveled against them refer to what supposedly happened during these meetings, and Pliny, governor of the province of Bithynia (in what is now Turkey), writing to the Emperor Trajan in A.D. 110 about the Christians he had arrested, spoke of them "meeting on a particular day before dawn and singing a hymn to Christ as though to a god," and then meeting again in the evening of the same day for a common meal. It was *the* way of knowing whether a particular person was a Christian or not and therefore an essential element; they could be recognized in this way just as the two disillusioned disciples recognized Jesus in the breaking of bread (Luke 24:35). The reason is quite simple. Paul uses the Greek word for church, *ekklesia,* in three ways, distinct but intimately linked together. First, as the term for the whole of the divine commonwealth as conceived, planned and brought into effect by God; then, as the local community, insofar as it is the embodiment in time and space of the first; then finally

as the liturgical get-together of the local community, insofar as by meeting together to celebrate the death of
the Lord, it realizes its own nature, its potentialities, to
the fullest extent and, at the same time, realizes (that is,
brings into effect), what the Church as a universal idea
implies. Thus Paul, in his first letter to the Corinth
community, can address them as "the Church (*ekklesia*)
of God which is at Corinth" and later, talking of the
weekly meeting, speak of them assembling together "as
a church (*ekklesia*)." We can understand perfectly, in
the light of this, why the author of the letter to the
Hebrews sees the failure of his readers to meet together
once a week as a sign of their losing their faith (Hebrews 10:25).

But why Sunday rather than any other day? The
meeting at Troas, during which Eutyches fell asleep,
took place, Luke tells us, "on the first day of the week
when we were gathered together to break bread." The
first day of the week is the first day after the Jewish
sabbath, the day on which Mary Magdalen made her
momentous journey to visit the sepulchre. The mysterious, heavenly liturgy in the Book of the Apocalypse
(Revelation) takes place "on the Lord's day" which is
the day when, as Ignatius Bishop of Antioch put it,
"our life had its rising." If we bear this in mind, it is
not difficult to see how our presence at the memorial
service of our Lord's death on the day of his resurrection takes us at once to the heart of what being a
Christian means. That is why Paul insists on this so
much, that is why his letters are addressed to his
Christians gathered together "as a Church." The weekly
meeting has to be the continued experience of the risen
Lord among us and a dramatic anticipation of the
whole purpose of the Christian life which is, in Paul's

phrase, "to attain to the resurrection from the dead" (Philippians 3:11).

This is the basic explanation, but it is evidently not enough to "go" to church, just to be there. It is clear that at Troas or Corinth or any other of the communities founded or visited by Paul, those present at the weekly session[1] were evidently not content to sink back into a restful anonymity, or settle down quietly behind a pillar to sleep out the great gap of time to the final blessing. Nor was their presence anything like that of the *ekklesia* or public assembly at Ephesus in the theater where "most of them did not know why they had come together." Not only did all take part in the prayers and hymns and listen to the Word of God (read in their own language), but all communicated at the passing round the table of the bread and the cup after the president of the meeting had finished the great prayer of thanksgiving.

Summarizing the essential elements in the life of the first Christians, Luke says: "They devoted themselves to the apostles' teaching and fellowship, to the breaking of bread and the prayers" (in Acts 2:42). Whether intentionally or not, these four points sum up not only their common life in the Christian community, but also what happens in the weekly meeting which is, in any case, supposed to be a mirror of that life. We have already seen how Paul's letters were written to be

[1] Not quite a happy word, since the early Christians stood for prayer, thus expressing better than we do the idea of an *ekklesia,* an assembly of the whole people, an active presence. Kneeling—and sometimes prostrating—was reserved for special penitentiary occasions. When the eucharist was still integrated into the community meal they reclined in the contemporary fashion, while for instruction and the "sermon" they presumably sat, to judge by the case of Eutyches.

read in the weekly assembly, and this would apply also to the instruction of the other apostles based on "all that Jesus began to do and teach." This corresponds to our Epistle and Gospel, God's Word to us as a community. As for the prayers, it is clear from the letters that Paul continually prayed for his Christians and that they offered up prayers at their meetings for him and for the needs of the moment, of others and of themselves. They also prayed the psalms, reprayed them we might say, in the light of the fulfillment of sacred history in Christ. The first meeting for prayer after Pentecost (Acts 4:24–31) consisted of a psalm and a Christian meditation on it, while Paul speaks more than once of his Christians singing "psalms and hymns and spiritual songs." It is not difficult to see how this corresponds in our service with the prayers beginning with the entry psalm (Introit) and ending with what we call the Postcommunion, though unfortunately the ancient "bidding" prayers have fallen out.[2]

One of the foremost purposes of the meeting is to be able to experience in a direct way the meaning of what Luke calls "fellowship." This comes from the consciousness of belonging to the one community of the redeemed, bound together in a union of deep charity, going beyond self-interest, and extending beyond the boundaries of the local community to the whole of the universal Church and of mankind. This latter was expressed in a concrete way by the collection

---

[2] The *Dominus Vobiscum* before the Offertory is followed by an invitation to pray but no prayer follows (except on Good Friday). The practice of "Bidding" prayers, preserved in the Anglican vernacular liturgy, was in use in the medieval Mass; they came after the sermon and were rounded off with the *Kyrie Eleison*.

(this is one element which was present right from the start!)—a financial contribution to help the mother Church in Jerusalem which was made, according to Paul's stipulation, "on the first day of every week" (I Corinthians 16:2). But this fellowship in the meeting is not just a fellowship between Christian and fellow-Christian; it is also a union of the whole community with Christ present in his death and resurrection, a *communion* therefore, and in fact Paul is the first to use this term, so familiar to us, of the sharing in the eucharist: "The cup of blessing which we bless, is it not a communion in the blood of Christ? The bread which we break, is it not a communion in the body of Christ?" (I Corinthians 10:16).

To go a step further. As everyone knows, having a meal together is one of the most ancient and best established ways of promoting companionship and mutual understanding. It is here that the sacramental idea is found at its deepest and its most human level— the craving to satisfy bodily hunger and thirst and the need for companionship. So here all share in a meal together with the risen Christ, just as he ate and drank with his friends "on the night he was betrayed." "Breaking bread" is the ordinary Jewish phrase for having a meal, but for Christians it became *the* meal which gives to those who take part a share in the sacrificial death of the Lord which they commemorate, and consequently a share in the new life that was his beyond the reach of death after the resurrection.

The Christian Out of Church

What we have been saying applies, however, only to one hour (and probably less) out of the hundred and

sixty-eight of the Christian's week. What then is the
relation between the Christian-in-church and the Chris-
tian-out-of-church? In trying to get at Paul's answer to
this question we come across an apparent contradiction.
On the one hand, the liturgical meeting is paramount,
to the extent that we can explain practically all the
terms Paul uses for "Christian" in relation to the active
presence at this meeting: to this he has been "called";
it is here that he becomes one with those who "call
upon the name of the Lord" and can be described as
"holy" by reason of the Spirit who is invisibly but
powerfully present, and "brother" on account of the
co-presence of those who share in that same Spirit. Yet
at the same time, paradoxically, Paul shows little interest in liturgy as it is usually understood; there is little of
the smell of incense and candle wax about his letters,
and the man who celebrated the eucharist on a sinking
ship in a storm among a crowd of terrified sailors might
have found the complicated rubrics of our solemn High
Mass quite a problem. We do not, in fact, think of him
easily as a priest, and he never mentions priests in his
letters; in fact the word never occurs in the New Testament of individual Christians.[3]

We get a clue toward a solution when we notice
that, in Paul's letters, the vocabulary of the Old Testament liturgical and sacrificial system is lifted from its

---

[3] It is used of *Jewish priests* such as Caiphas; of *pagan
priests,* like the ones who wanted to sacrifice to Paul and
Barnabas in Lycaonia; of *the whole people of God* (in Revelation 1:6; 5:10; 20:6; cf. I Peter 2:5–9) but always with reference to the Assembly of Israel in the Old Testament as a
sacrificial community (see Exodus 19:6). According to the
Letter to the Hebrews, the risen and glorified Christ is the one
priest of the new dispensation and all Christians share in this
sacerdotal office, if in different degrees.

original context and used of Christian existence in general and the ministry in particular. Thus he tells the Romans that he *worship*s God in his spirit through his work of going about spreading the Christian good news (Romans 1:9) and he invites the same community to offer their bodies as a living *sacrifice*—a spiritual *worship*—in contrast to the liturgical worship, understood in the narrow sense, of Judaism (12:1). When he feels that his death is near, he speaks of his life being "poured out as a *libation* upon the *sacrificial offering* of your faith" (Philippians 2:17; cf. II Timothy 4:6).

We might put it another way by saying that for Paul, both before and after his conversion, the whole point of religion and, indeed, of existence on this earth, is to come into God's presence, what he calls "access" to God. For Jews in the Old Testament period and beyond, this was possible only through ministers of worship and in an act of worship; hence the importance of the Temple liturgy and, in particular, the climax of that liturgy in the great Day of Expiation (they call it *Yom Kippur*) when the high priest, this once in the whole year, entered the inner sanctuary, the Holy of Holies, and made expiation for the sins of the whole people. This was *the* access to God, and naturally it was only for Jews since all Gentiles were ritually impure and could not "come near" to God. On his visit to Jerusalem, where we left him in the last section, Paul was almost lynched for having, supposedly, brought an Ephesian, Trophimus by name, into the inner Temple court beyond the wall to pass which meant death to any Gentile.[4] He is no doubt thinking of this incident

---

[4] Two of the inscribed notices warning Gentiles have been recovered by archaeologists. The inscription reads: "No

some three or four years later when, writing to the fellow-citizens of Trophimus, he says: "In Christ Jesus you who once were far off have been brought near in the blood of Christ. For he is our peace, who has made us both one, and has broken down the dividing wall of hostility" (Ephesians 2:13-14).

The one access to God now is in the Church, which lives from the great act of reconciliation and expiation revealed in the death and resurrection of the Lord, and in the church service which commemorates that act and applies it to our lives. What we do in church is, therefore, a means of expressing and actualizing what our belonging to the Church means.

Living Your Baptism

One thing that strikes us in reading Acts and Paul's letters is how informal and spontaneous the Christian life is in contrast with our own practice. This is true even of the sacraments and the two great sacraments of baptism and the eucharist on which that life is grounded. We have seen this already with regard to the latter: nothing really fixed, great freedom in the choice of prayers, no manuals or rubrics required; it could be celebrated in the house of any Christian or even in the unpropitious circumstances of a shipwreck, as we have seen. The same was true of baptism: an official from the Sudan on a diplomatic mission receives a brief instruction and is baptized at once in the first pool or river he and Philip come to; a jailer is instructed briefly in a dark prison just after an earthquake and baptized

stranger is permitted to enter within the screen and enclosure round the Holy Place. Whoever is caught will himself be responsible for his death which will follow."

at once; and in one case the Holy Spirit is given, manifesting his presence in external signs, even before the rite of baptism is performed.

This may appear to us today to have disadvantages, but at least it has the advantage of showing us what is central to the whole Christian life—the mystery of the Holy Spirit manifested through these signs in freedom and power, the mystery accepted joyfully in faith and complete commitment of the whole of life. This was effected in baptism and it is here that one of the greatest and most subtle differences can be seen between the "then" and the "now." At that time the order was conversion and then baptism, while now, with infant baptism the standard form, this order is reversed with the result, in many cases, that the conversion part is forgotten. We can even go through life with a vague idea left over from the way people may have spoken to us when we were small children that once our soul had been made white in baptism (as if it had been dipped in some solution) everything was all right. According to Paul, on the contrary, the task remains of making our own the faith which holy Church put at our disposal then in the person of the godparent.

What is rather frightening about the "then" in this respect is the extent to which it was taken for granted that sin, moral evil and disorder were out of the question for the Christian after being baptized. We could recall the, for us, incredibly severe discipline of the early centuries in regard to those guilty of grave public sin, and the controversy about rebaptism in the case of sins like that of giving way to temporary apostasy under pressure during the persecutions. One New Testament writer states: "It is impossible to restore again to repentance those who have once been enlightened"

(Hebrews 6:4—this last is a synonym for "baptized") and Paul himself states quite simply:

"How can we who died to sin still live in it?"
and he continues, giving the reason: "Do you not know that all of us who have been baptized into Christ Jesus have been baptized into his death? We were buried, therefore, with him by baptism into death, so that, as Christ was raised from the dead by the glory of the Father, we too might walk in newness of life" (Romans 6:2–4).

Our faith is not, therefore, as so many think, a moral code: the moral part is simply the necessary result of living in the mystery, in this newness of life, this new creation. If we are convinced of this, we can leave behind a moral life based on fear and inhibition and begin to live in freedom and responsibility—what Paul calls the freedom of the children of God. Again, this springs from the moment of baptism: "You did not receive (in baptism) the spirit of slavery to fall back into fear, but you have received the spirit of sonship. When we cry "Abba! Father!" it is the Spirit himself bearing witness with our spirit that we are the children of God" (Romans 8:15–16).

These are the principles and this is the ideal, but, despite Paul's rhetorical question, we *do* continue to live in sin and it does not take a very deep reading of the correspondence to see that this was true of baptized Christians right from the beginning. The divine prerogative of forgiving sins is exercised by certain men who, however, perform this function within the community and, in a certain sense, on behalf of the community so that we are forgiven as members of the whole body. In the early Church, as we know from *The Teaching of the Twelve Apostles,* the confession could in fact be made publicly to the community in the weekly assembly, probably before the eucharist. This was an excellent and deeply Christian practice, but we should probably prefer our own method with all its attendant difficulties! In whatever way it is practiced, we should think of it as a return to baptism and the wholehearted commitment which this implies. Similarly, all the other sacraments are intimately connected with the central mystery of the communication of the divine life as touching our human existence at certain crucial points. Indeed, everything which is in the Church, all the externals which sometimes make it hard for us to go to the center, the legal and juridical aspects, the administration and codification, exist only in view of what was then and is now the one thing necessary: God coming to us in Jesus and our response in faith.

Part VII
The Last Phase

WE left Paul in Jerusalem in the autumn of the year 58. If he had already described himself as a man condemned to death and dying every day, he was entering now on a period of extreme peril from which he finally extricated himself only by appealing to the ultimate authority in Rome.

Appeal to Caesar

We have to remember that Paul arrived when unrest was rapidly building up to the climax of the outbreak of civil war and revolt in 66, and he himself was at first mistaken for a wanted messiah who had shortly before led an armed attack on the city from the direction of the Mount of Olives, in which about four hundred had been killed. It was also Pentecost, one of the three great pilgrim feasts when the city was crowded and trouble could be expected—one recalls the pilgrims whose blood, as Luke tells us in his Gospel (13:1), Pilate had mingled with that of their sacrifices. There is also more than one point of comparison between what happened to Paul and what had happened to his Lord on that Passover almost thirty years before: the same kind of accusation, the fury of the mob, the hearing before the Roman governor, the Jewish high council and a member of the Herod family.

The trouble started with the Trophimus episode

referred to above. Paul was saved from lynching at the last moment by the Roman troops who hurried him into Antonia Tower. Here we see Paul at his best, when his fortunes seemed at their lowest ebb. He insisted on making one last attempt to clear himself and turned on the barrack steps and spoke to them in their own language. His argument was the same, and remained so to the end: what he had traveled the world proclaiming was not a new religion; it was their faith, and now everybody's, brought to its fulfillment in the resurrection of Jesus, "the first to rise from the dead" (16:23)— therefore the beginning of the new age. When he was shouted down, the tribune and his men took him inside to have him flogged—the usual preliminary to an interrogation when any difficulty in extracting information was foreseen. Once again, and at the last moment, his Roman citizenship saved him. The evident pride with which he mentions this shows us that there was no false meekness or humility about Paul.

The same characteristic was seen in the appearance before the Jewish Council on the following morning. The citizen of no mean city, the Roman born, flared up hotly when the high priest ordered him to be struck in defiance of legal procedure; and even though he at once humbly withdrew what he had said, his words were to be fulfilled not long after when Ananias was deposed, later to be killed by a band of Zealots. Thus the meeting got off to a lively start and soon broke up in confusion as a result of Paul deliberately splitting the Seventy by setting the Pharisee element against the Sadducee in staking his claim to orthodoxy on the resurrection of the dead—a doctrine basic to Pharisee theology but rejected by the more traditional and fundamentalist Sadducees. This certainly showed Paul's resource and *sangfroid* in difficult circumstances, but it was not just a trick. The resurrection of Jesus was in reality the fulfillment of what Paul, as a Pharisee, had always believed in, and this forms the climax also of his speeches before Felix and Agrippa where there was no need for the same kind of expediency.

The outline of what happened is easily told. The day after the farcical ending to the Council meeting, a group of more than forty Zealots made a vow not to eat or drink until they had killed Paul, and then set about preparing an ambush. These extremists, according to Josephus Flavius, a Jewish deserter to the Romans who wrote the history of the war, were the chief cause of the outbreak of violence, and had recently begun to step up their campaign of provocation and armed resistance.[1] Fortunately, however, Paul's nephew got wind of the plot and revealed it to the tribune who sent Paul under an extremely strong escort the sixty-five miles to the procurator's headquarters in Caesarea, leaving at 9 p.m. in order to forestall any countermeasures. After riding all that night and the following day, they were presented to the procurator, Antonius Felix, who arranged for the trial to take place at Caesarea as soon as his accusers should arrive. They did so after five days and this time, admonished by their tactical failure a week earlier, brought a lawyer with them. After the usual flattering overtures to the "most excellent Felix," the lawyer accused Paul of being a dangerous religious agitator, hoping that the procurator

---

[1] Paul himself was mistaken for the leader of a band of these *sicarii* or "dagger-men" (from the Latin *sica*=dagger). The view that Judas Iscariot should really read "Judas the sicarius" (by a change of consonant position called "metathesis") is hardly probable.

would feel obliged to take sudden and drastic action as he had a reputation for doing. He did not do so, however, but adjourned the session and kept Paul in custody until the end of his period of office. What happened to the Zealots and their vow in the meantime we are not told.

The new governor, Porcius Festus, perhaps wishing to compensate for some of the bad feeling caused by his predecessor, took a more conciliatory line with Paul's Jewish accusers and tried to pass him over to their high Council. This left Paul with only one alternative, one he had no doubt thought over deeply during his eighteen months in prison: he must refer his case to the court of supreme appeal in Rome. It was this or death. His appeal was accepted, as it had to be, and there was, therefore, no question of further legal proceedings once that step had been taken; he was safe for the time being. The arrival of king Agrippa II in Caesarea a few days later gave Paul an opportunity to expound his cause before the secular head of the Jewish people, which he did in one of his most fervent and eloquent witnesses to the power of God now revealed in the risen Lord. There is in these trials and hearings something very appropriate to the situation of the world faced with the call to decision which the Christian faith forces upon it; in fact we are left wondering more than once who is on trial, Paul or his hearers. We know something about these men and women as we imagine them sitting in the audience hall and wonder what was passing through their minds. Felix, the ex-slave, morose and capricious as a ruler, seems to have been definitely interested and may have continued listening to Paul during the remaining months before his recall. His wife Drusilla, a pleasure loving divorcee, daughter of Herod Agrippa whose murder of James is recorded in Acts, may have been responsible for the suggestion of keeping Paul in prison in the hope of him buying his freedom with a bribe. Her brother and sister Herod Agrippa II and Berenice (Veronica is a later form of the same name) were also likely descendants of the Herod of the Gospels. The former, cordially detested by the Jews especially the priests, listened with a detached, superficial kind of interest and brushed off Paul's direct appeal to him with an embarrassed joke: "If you keep going, you'll soon be thinking you've made a Christian of me!" His sister, cousin of the notorious Salome, had been twice married before her fifteenth birthday, became a byword for profligacy and ended up in the company of Titus, Roman conqueror of Jerusalem. For all of these and for Festus, on whom Paul's words were completely lost, the moment of decision passed and very likely never came again.

The Fourth Shipwreck

The voyage to Rome began late in the year in a small coaster which put in at the ports along the coast of Asia Minor. Paul was allowed on parole at Sidon to visit the Christian community there and would shortly afterwards have sailed past the coast of his native Cilicia, wondering no doubt whether he would ever see it again. At the port of Myra they changed to one of the big ships of the Egyptian grain fleet bound for Italy which made slow and ponderous progress round the Island of Rhodes and across to the small port of Fair Havens in Crete, where Titus was afterwards to be bishop. Since, as Luke tells us, *Yom Kippur* had already come and gone, which meant that they were in the period of the autumn equinoctial storms, they held a council of war as to whether it was worth the risk to continue the journey or put up and winter where they were. Paul, as a distinguished Roman citizen although a prisoner, seems to have been admitted to this meeting and strongly advised against continuing. He had been shipwrecked three times already and had spent a whole day and a night in an open boat, so he knew what he was talking about (see II Corinthians 11:25), but the centurion, whose word was law, decided to back the captain's evident desire to push on, at least until they could find a more suitable place to winter in.

They therefore made a run for the larger harbor of Phoenix, near the western tip of the island, but were caught by a strong northeaster and, not having the sail to tack, were driven helplessly towards the African coast. Here Paul showed himself the man of action by keeping up their spirits and, at one critical moment, preventing the Egyptian crew from abandoning the rest to their fate and taking to the large ship's boat. After a fortnight of drifting, having jettisoned the precious cargo and all the heavy gear, they struck a shoal off Malta and the ship broke up. Normally the prisoners would have been killed to prevent their escaping or overpowering their captors, but some kind of a friendship seems to have sprung up between Julius the centurion and Paul, and the former gave everyone the chance to make land.

We cannot fail to note how, even in the most difficult circumstances Paul is always, in his own phrase, an ambassador for Christ. The same goes for the three months of enforced residence in the island. Luke tells, with his usual quiet irony, of how Paul, helping to make a fire on the shore since it was cold and raining, was bitten by a viper, and the *barbaroi* [2] immediately jumped to the conclusion that he must be a murderer and that this was the goddess Justice catching up with him; when, however, he just carried on gathering sticks and nothing happened to him, they changed their minds and decided he was a god (this was the second time for Paul!). Here, as elsewhere, the sick were healed and the power of the Lord Jesus made manifest.

The End of the Road

Another Alexandrian ship, the *Castor and Pollux,* bound for the port of Pozzuoli in the Bay of Naples, took them aboard. They stayed three days in Syracuse where later there was to be a flourishing Christian church, and from there, after putting in at Rhegium (Reggio) on the tip of the toe of Italy, they reached Pozzuoli in three days. Paul must have taken a long look at Vesuvius smoking as they warped into port; just over two years later it was to erupt and destroy a good part of the large provincial town of Pompeii, a prelude to the total destruction sixteen years afterwards.[3] The Christian community which they found in

---

[2] For a cultured Hellenist like Luke, *barbaros* meant anyone beyond the area where Greek was spoken and where Greek culture prevailed.

[3] In A.D. 63 a large part of the town was destroyed. Some rebuilding was done but the great eruption of August 24th, A.D. 79, covered both Pompeii and nearby Herculaneum in a deep layer of incandescent ash. If the crosses discovered in both towns are definitely Christian and the *Sator* acrostic really contains an anagram on the Lord's prayer, this would merely confirm the impression we get from Acts of the existence of small Christian communities in Italy before Paul's arrival.

Pozzuoli, no doubt to their delighted surprise, invited them to stay for a week. The seaports of the Mediterranean were among the first centers to have Christian communities, for obvious reasons. They probably began on a very small scale, following the Jewish pattern of setting up a synagogue with a quorum of ten and then attracting new members. We do not know how big the church was in this major port, or whether they were familiar with Paul's Roman letter written some three years before. At any rate, he had a chance of recovering from the exhausting sea trip and resting before the last stage of the journey on foot. Christians from the capital ventured the forty-five miles to the Appian Market on the Brindisi Road to meet the travelers and accompany them on the last day or two of their journey. After a stop at Three Taverns some ten miles further along to have their animals seen to, and perhaps take hot drinks at a *thermopolium,* they continued along the old Appian Road over the broad *campagna,* past the lakes of Nemi and Albano surrounded with fashionable villas, past the tombs and the magnificent Claudian aqueduct recently completed, entering the city by the Capena Gate. We can only imagine Paul's feelings at that moment, his long road having led him to the center of the world.

Luke tells us that Paul's first thought was to get in touch with the Jewish community and explain his position. The reception was distinctly cool and few were convinced by his line of argument. He was under close surveillance but was, it seems, allowed to rent a house, probably somewhere near the barracks of the Pretorian Guard (where the university now stands) and receive visitors. This continued for two years and, since Luke's story ends at this point, we may suppose that

Paul was set free as Agrippa and Festus had evidently foreseen he would be. We do not know whether Luke ever continued his story and in the absence of sound documentation, are thrown back on conjecture. Presuming that the so-called Captivity Epistles were written during this time, it appears that he was able to keep up his connections with the churches of Asia and Macedonia. Thus we know that a certain Epaphroditus brought him a gift-parcel and probably money from the Christians of Philippi: Lydia, Evodia, Syntyche and the rest, and returned with a beautifully written letter of thanks. Tychicus was sent to Ephesus and Colossae with letters and to act as escort for Onesimos the runaway slave, bearing with him a covering note to Philemon his owner, a rich Christian of Colossae whose house was used for the weekly meeting. From the request to the latter to have a guest room prepared for him, we might assume that Paul saw his release as imminent and was planning a return to Asia.

Whether he was able to keep to this plan we do not know, and in fact have no certain sources of knowledge for the last few years. These were the years which saw the situation in Palestine get gradually out of hand and slide into the terrible war of extermination which was just beginning when Paul met his death, while in Rome the last of the Caesars, finally freed from Seneca's influence, was beginning to show up in his true colors. Paul may, during this troubled period, have fulfilled his ambition of preaching the Word in Spain (see Romans 15:24)—Clement, head of the Roman Church at the end of the century, says that he went "to the limits of the west"—he may have visited Crete (Titus 1:5), Greece (Titus 3:12) and Macedonia (I Timothy 1:3) and started a mission in Gaul by sending Crescens (II

Timothy 4:10). Putting together the scanty indications that we find in the "pastoral" letters—the two to Timothy and the one to Titus—and in later tradition, we may suppose that his enemies caught up with him obliging him a second time to claim a hearing in the imperial court of appeal. It may be, as some have supposed, that he was betrayed by that Alexander the coppersmith who, as he tells Timothy (II Timothy 4:14), had done him great harm. At any rate, there was little chance of him escaping a second time. Already members of the "pernicious superstition," as Tacitus calls it, had suffered death as convenient scapegoats for the great fire which broke out on July 18th, 64 and destroyed most of the city.

Presuming that the letter as we have it is from his hand, the last word is in the second of the two which he wrote to his disciple, Timothy. Reading it we see that there was no conventional happy ending for Paul. He who had renounced the joy and fulfillment of marriage and a settled life, who had worked for his living day in and day out so as not to be a burden on those to whom he communicated the greatest gift of all, who had traveled most of the roads of the empire with an old cloak and a few scrolls for his luggage, was left to die practically alone. "At my first defense no one took my part," he writes; "all deserted me. . . . Luke alone is with me." Later writers tell us that he was condemned and beheaded some two or three miles out of the city along the road to the port of Ostia, beyond where the great church which bears his name now stands. He had described death as "the last enemy" and always seen it as within the mystery of the death and new life of the Lord: "We have this treasure in earthern vessels, to show that the transcendent power belongs to God and not to us" (II Corinthians 4:7).

This was a new beginning, not an end.

Chronological
Table

FIXING a chronological sequence for Paul's life is notoriously difficult, not only on account of the lack of reliable material for the early period down to the death of Stephen and the last period after Luke's story ends, but also because of the difficulty of synchronizing with the absolutely fixed chronology of world history at that time. For this latter we have only the tenure of office of Gallio at Corinth, known to be from 51 to 52 from the Delphic inscription, the famine during the reign of Claudius, probably 46 to 49, and the end of Felix's procuratorship, 59 to 60. All the dates that follow, therefore, are uncertain, though there is now considerable agreement for the middle period.

10	Birth
	Early Years in Tarsus
28	Student in Jerusalem
36	Persecution of Hellenist Christians
	Conversion
36–39	Ministry in Damascus and "Arabia"
39	First Visit to the Jerusalem Church
39–44	In Syria and Cilicia
44	Invited to Antioch by Barnabas

45–49 Antioch Mission
49–50 Jerusalem meeting(s) and Antioch incident with
         Peter
50–52 Mission into Europe; Two Years at Corinth
                            I, II Thessalonians
53–58 The Ephesus Mission   *Galatians*
54–57 In Ephesus and Province of Asia
                            I, II Corinthians
57–58 Visit to Corinth   *Romans*
58   Arrival in Jerusalem
58–60 Prison in Caesarea
60–61 Voyage to Rome
61   Prison in Rome   *Philippians, Ephesians,*
                            Colossians, Philemon
         Last Years—Asia, Macedonia, Achaia, Spain?
                            I Timothy? Titus?
67(64?) Prison in Rome—Execution   *II Timothy?*

Suggestions for Further Reading

Life

Ricciotti, *Paul the Apostle* (Bruce, 1961). This translation from the Italian (1946, first edition) covers most aspects of Paul's life and background.

Dodd, *The Meaning of Paul for Today* (Meridian). This short study of Paul's thought, first published in 1920, gives great and merited importance to the idea of community and the Church. The author, a Congregationalist, is one of the leading British New Testament scholars.

Tresmontant, *Saint Paul and the Mystery of Christ* (Longmans, 1957). The biographical part of this *Men of Wisdom* paperback is presented in a lively way and the cosmic aspects of the Apostle's thought are stressed.

Deissmann, *Paul: A Study in Social and Religious History* (Smith, Peter, 1958). First published in 1912, this study remains today as fresh and stimulating (and controversial) as when first published.

Knox, R. A., *St. Paul's Gospel* (Sheed & Ward, 1953).

Background

Kee and Young, *The Living World of the New Testament* (Darton, Longman & Todd, 1960, second edition). The section on Paul (pp. 207–309) is probably not the best in the book though freshly written and full of good ideas. He rejects the Pastorals.

Cadbury, *The Book of Acts in History* (Humanities, 1955). Interesting source material; gleanings from a lifetime's work on Acts.

Barrett, *The New Testament Background: Selected Documents* (Torchbooks, 1961). A well-chosen selection covering the three "areas" of Paul's background: Roman, Greek, Jewish.

Finegan, *Light from the Ancient Past* (Princeton, 2nd ed., 1959). Pp. 331–384 bear directly on Paul's background but there are other sections, for example on writing materials, the archaeology of early Christian Rome, etc., which are useful and interesting.

Ramsay, *St. Paul the Traveller and Roman Citizen* (Baker, 1960). This vintage volume (and any of the others of Ramsay which the reader can obtain) is recommended as an interesting and highly personal approach to the Apostle. The case of a man being completely won over!

Morton, *In the Steps of St. Paul* (Dodd, 1966). Always interesting and some good photographs.

There are no popular, "novelized" lives known to us which we can recommend. For an imaginative penetration of the age there are quite a number of good novels of which we could mention:

George Moore, *The Brook Kerith* (Liveright, or Tudor).

Robert Graves, *I, Claudius* (Modern Lib.).

Bulwer-Lytton, *The Last Days of Pompeii* (Collins; Dutton).

Thought

Cerfaux, *Christ in the Theology of Saint Paul* (Herder & Herder) and *The Church in the Theology of Saint Paul* (Herder & Herder). No doubt his *Le Chrétien dans la Théologie paulinienne* (Paris, Cerf, 1962) will soon appear in English to complete the trilogy which, in most respects, supersedes the classic work of Prat on the Theology of St. Paul.

Dodd, *The Apostolic Preaching and Its Development* (Harper, 1936). Excellent explanation of the *Kerygma* which, as has been brought out in the study, is indispensable for understanding the theology of the epistles.

Durrwell, *The Resurrection* (Sheed & Ward, 1960). A compendious study of what is the starting point and center of Paul's theology.

Davies, *Paul and Rabbinical Judaism* (S.P.C.K.) (Seabury, 2nd ed., 1955). More advanced and technical, but invaluable in presenting Paul as first and foremost a convert Pharisee.

Parkes, *Jesus, Paul and the Jews* (S.C.M., 1936). The wider Jewish historical and religious background.

Commentaries on individual letters and the key passages quoted or referred to in this study will be found in the English translation of the *Jerusalem Bible* (Doubleday, 1966), together with valuable introductions and notes.

New Testament Summaries of
The Christian Message

1. *The Pentecost Sermon (Acts 2:14–36)*

The presence of the Spirit, shown in the "speaking with tongues," is the beginning of the last age spoken of by the prophets and is for all the moment of decision. It begins with the life and death of Jesus of Nazareth:
— mighty works, wonders and signs *which God did through him*=the public ministry
— delivered up=the betrayal by Judas
— you crucified and killed=passion and death
— but God raised him up=the resurrection which is demonstrated by scripture proof (Psalms 16, 132, 110) and by witnesses to the Lord after his resurrection
— exalted at the right hand of God=the ascension
— poured out the Spirit=Pentecost as the baptism of the Church.

2. *After the Healing at the Beautiful Gate (Acts 3:13–25)*

The whole redemptive event is referred to as the *glorification of Jesus* which is the term used in the

Gospel of St. John, and the one who glorifies him is the God who acts throughout the whole course of sacred history.

— you killed the Author of Life
— but God raised him from the dead.

Here we find some amplification of the basic structure: Jesus is "the Servant" of the Isaian prophecies (especially Isaiah 52–53); the reference to Pilate (later in the Creed); the fulfillment of the promise to Abraham and of the prophecies.

3. *Before the Council (Acts 5:29–32)*

— you killed by hanging him on a tree
— the God of our fathers raised Jesus
— God exalted him at his right hand=ascension
— we are witnesses . . . and so is the Holy Spirit whom God has given=Pentecost.

Stephen and the Hellenist-Christian Position (Acts 7)

This is in fact a reinterpretation of the whole of Old Testament history and differs from the preceding in that Jesus, "the Righteous One," is mentioned only right at the end (v. 52), though present implicitly throughout. The attack is against the materialistic attachment to the Land and the Temple (both of which they were shortly to lose) which leads on to the forces behind the death of Christ:

— Abraham, Isaac, Jacob—they did not possess the Land
— Joseph and Israel in Egypt—still all they had of the Land was a tomb, a burial place

— Moses guided by the God of the fathers—one long story of opposition by his people=type of Jesus; Exodus type of his death and redemption
— Apostasy of Aaron—David—Solomon and the Temple.

Paul

1. *At Damascus (Acts 9:20–22)*

The essentials of sacred history, the bridge between the old and new is included in the one formula
— "Jesus is the Christ"=messiah; the fulfillment of the promises.

2. *In the Synagogue at Antioch in Pisidia (Acts 13:16–41)*

— Exodus from Egypt as act of God
— forty years in the desert
— Settlement in Canaan
— Judges
— Monarchy: Saul—David—Jesus of the dynasty of David
— Ministry of John Baptist
— Ministry of Jesus
— *they* asked Pilate to have him killed . . . laid him in a tomb
— but *God* raised him from the dead; the resurrection is the climax: "We bring you the good news that what God has promised to the fathers this he has fulfilled to us their children by raising Jesus" (v. 33).

Here we have the most complete scheme so far; note how there is no break between the old and the new, precisely because it is the same God who operates.

3. *To the Christians of Corinth*
   (I Corinthians 15:3–8)

— Christ died for our sins *according to the scriptures*
— he was buried
— he was raised on the third day *according to the scriptures*
— appearances of the risen Lord: to Peter and the Twelve; to more than 500; to James and the Twelve; to Paul.

This is the essential gist of Paul's message or Kerygma, which he had received (the technical term for the tradition) and which he had to pass on unchanged. The resurrection is again (and always) the climax.